I0617254

MY

ActingSmarter

PAPERBACK PLANNER

Acting Smarter

Planning and tracking your way to the top

This Planner Belongs To:

_____

Plan and prepare your life today to set yourself up for success and prosperity.

-Lydia Nicole

Copyright©2023 Lydia Nicole

All rights reserved. No parts of this planner may be reproduced, copied, distributed, or otherwise exploited in whole or in part without the prior written permission of the author.

ISBN: 979-8-9865143-9-0   (Paperback)

Printed in the United States of America.

Second printing, 2023

Lydia Nicole Media
10153 1/2 Riverside Drive #143
Toluca Lake, CA 91602
Email: FaithHolder@actingsmarternow.com
www.actingsmarternow.com

WELCOME

Dear Actor,

I have made my own planners since 2007. In my homemade planners, I put my vision boards, my goals, my achievements, my ideas, my affirmations, and my dreams. I used them to keep track of my meetings, my auditions, my network contacts, and hit lists of people I want to work with and the productions I want to be a part of. I also write my prayers and track which have been answered in it.

I use my planner to keep me organized, focused and clear about where I am, where I've been, and where I want to go. They help me to reflect, review, and reignite myself.

My prayer is that this planner will do the same for you and will assist you in becoming more intentional, committed, and consistent as you strive to have a magnificent career.

I dedicate this planner to you, the courageous one who seeks to turn dreams into reality.

This planner was created to help you push past fears, distractions, and disappointments, and keep you steady in the pursuit of your acting career. I know how easy it can be to block your blessings and not reach your dreams because you are overwhelmed by the nonsense life brings.

I encourage you to continue to dream big. Write them down, think, see, feel, and own them. Habakkuk 2:2-3 tells us to write down our vision. Believe God to bring it all to you bigger and better than you could ever hope or imagine. Focus only on God's blessings for you and not on temporary trials or tribulations. As a child of the King you are blessed to be a blessing to everyone around you, but you can only do it if you are on your path with intentionality. And in case no one has told you, you are a winner and a champion. So, walk confidently in the God who created you. Know that God would not give you gifts and talents and then not let you use them. That is not the God we serve. I am so proud of you for going after your dreams! Keep going after your heart's desires. Don't let the critics in your head or the world keep you from your destiny. Go prepared, give it your best, and create unforgettable characters that inspire the world.

Love,

Lydia Nicole

HOW TO USE

USE THIS PLANNER TO:

- Dream your future, and set goals with clear intentions
- Create a plan to achieve those goals
- Keep yourself accountable to make your dreams and goals happen
- Organize your professional and personal life
- Keep track of your meetings
- Keep track of meetings with your representation
- Keep track of your submissions and auditions
- Keep track of your money
- Expand your knowledge and growth
- Establish and build your support team
- Build healthy industry relationships
- Be consistent
- Practice daily self-care
- Practice daily spiritual practice (gratitude, prayers, affirmations)
- Practice living your best life daily

VIDEO BONUS MATERIALS

Below is the link to access the video bonus material accompanying this book.

https://www.lydianicole.com/plannerbonus

GOALS ACCOMPLISHED

IN THE LAST YEAR

GOALS

TO ACCOMPLISH THIS YEAR

GOALS
TO ACCOMPLISH THIS YEAR

JANUARY

ACTING PRIORITIES

LIFE PRIORITIES

MONTHLY BUDGET

INCOME

INCOME-1	
OTHER INCOME	
INCOME-2	
BUDGET	

EXPENSES

MONTHLY LIVING

ACTING

BILL TO BE PAID	DUE DATE	AMOUNT	PAID	NOTES
_____	_____	_____	_____	
_____	_____	_____	_____	
_____	_____	_____	_____	
_____	_____	_____	_____	
_____	_____	_____	_____	
_____	_____	_____	_____	
_____	_____	_____	_____	
_____	_____	_____	_____	
_____	_____	_____	_____	

MONTHLY SUMMARY

TOTAL INCOME	TOTAL EXPENSES	DIFFERENCE

JANUARY

M	T	W	T

Notes

MONTHLY PLANNER

F	S	S

Acting Priorities

_____
_____
_____
_____
_____
_____
_____
_____

Career Priorities

_____
_____
_____
_____
_____
_____
_____
_____

Life Priorities

_____
_____
_____
_____
_____
_____
_____
_____

Positive Thoughts/Prayers/Affirmations

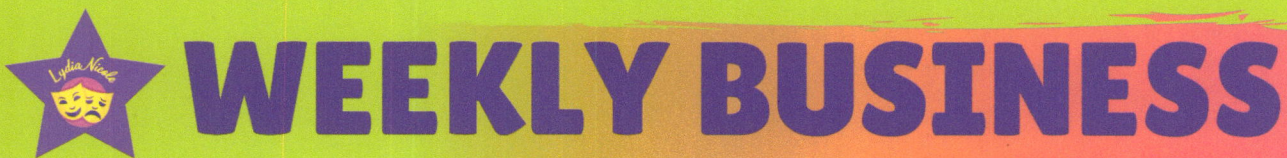

WEEKLY BUSINESS

ACTING   **BOOKINGS**   **PROJECTS**

SUNDAY

MONDAY

TUESDAY

WEDNESDAY

THURSDAY

FRIDAY

SATURDAY

THOUGHTS

WEEKLY BUSINESS

ACTING **BOOKINGS** **PROJECTS**

SUNDAY

MONDAY

TUESDAY

WEDNESDAY

THURSDAY

FRIDAY

SATURDAY

THOUGHTS

WEEKLY BUSINESS

ACTING　　　　**BOOKINGS**　　　　**PROJECTS**

SUNDAY

MONDAY

TUESDAY

WEDNESDAY

THURSDAY

FRIDAY

SATURDAY

THOUGHTS

WEEKLY BUSINESS

ACTING **BOOKINGS** **PROJECTS**

SUNDAY

MONDAY

TUESDAY

WEDNESDAY

THURSDAY

FRIDAY

SATURDAY

THOUGHTS

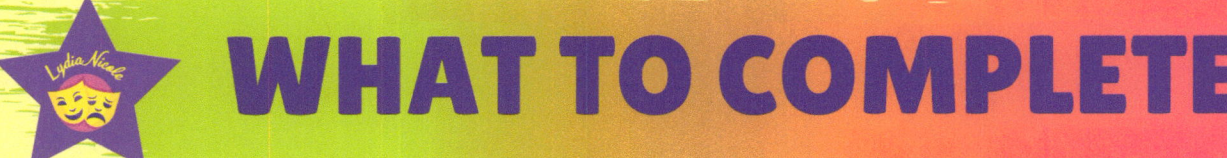

WHAT TO COMPLETE

LEAVE FOR LATER

AUDITION TRACKER

Date:_____

- ■ Self Tape
- ■ In-Person Audition
- ■ Request
- ■ Zoom
- ■ Callback
- ■ Sides
- ■ Producers
- ■ Script

Number of callbacks ☐   ■ Booked it

MY MOOD: 🙂 🥰 🙄 😎 🤔 😊 🤪 😴 😢 🥶 😡 😠

Contact Info

Address
_____
_____
_____

Email
_____
_____

Cell Phone
_____
_____

Wardrobe/Hair/Make-Up
*Include selfie of yourself before audition

_____
_____
_____

Project / Title / Role

_____
_____

Production Company

Director / Writer

Casting

Casting Director
_____
_____

Casting Assoc.
_____
_____

Casting Asst.
_____

AUDITION TRACKER

Date:_____

- ■ Self Tape
- ■ In-Person Audition
- ■ Request
- ■ Zoom
- ■ Callback
- ■ Sides
- ■ Producers
- ■ Script

Number of callbacks ▢   ■ Booked it

MY MOOD: 😌 🥰 🥺 😎 🤔 😊 🤪 😴 😢 🥶 😤 😠

Contact Info

Address_____

_____

_____

_____

Email

_____

_____

_____

Cell Phone

_____

_____

Wardrobe/Hair/Make-Up

*Include selfie of yourself before audition

_____

_____

_____

_____

Project / Title / Role

_____

_____

Production Company

Director / Writer

Casting

Casting Director

_____

_____

Casting Assoc.

_____

_____

Casting Asst.

AUDITION TRACKER

Date:_____

- 🟩 Self Tape
- 🟩 In-Person Audition
- 🟩 Request
- 🟩 Zoom
- 🟩 Callback
- 🟩 Sides
- 🟩 Producers
- 🟩 Script

Number of callbacks [ ]   🟩 Booked it

MY MOOD: 🙂 🥰 😳 😎 🤔 🫢 🤪 😴 😢 🥶 😠 😡

Contact Info

Address
_____
_____
_____
_____

Email
_____
_____
_____

Cell Phone
_____
_____

Wardrobe/Hair/Make-Up
_____
*Include selfie of yourself before audition
_____
_____
_____
_____

Project / Title / Role
_____
_____

Production Company

Director / Writer

Casting

Casting Director
_____

Casting Assoc.
_____

Casting Asst.
_____

AGENT/MANAGER TRACKER

Name	Title	Birthday
_____	_____	_____
_____	_____	_____
_____	_____	_____

Address
_____
_____
_____

Cell Phone   Email

_____   _____
_____   _____
_____   _____

Best day and time to contact
_____
_____

Other important information

AGENT/MANAGER TRACKER

DAY CALLED /VISITED	PURPOSE	OUTCOME	NOTES

MY MOOD:

DAY CALLED /VISITED	PURPOSE	OUTCOME

MY MOOD:

DAY CALLED /VISITED	PURPOSE	OUTCOME

MY MOOD:

DAY CALLED /VISITED	PURPOSE	OUTCOME

MY MOOD:

CALLED INTO SAY UNAVAILABLE	FROM	UNTIL
DATE:	DATE:	DATE:

MY MOOD:

INDUSTRY CONTACT TRACKER

Agent Connection

Name/ Agency   Date Contacted

_____

Contacted:
☐ Call   ☐ Email   ☐ Text   ☐ Postcard   ☐ Other_____

Discussed:
_____
_____
_____

Casting Director Connection

Name/ Company   Date Contacted

_____

Contacted:
☐ Call   ☐ Email   ☐ Text   ☐ Postcard   ☐ Other_____

Discussed:
_____
_____
_____

Industry Connection
(Director, Producer, Showrunner, Exec. Assistant, etc.)
Name/ Position/Company   Date Contacted

_____

Contacted:
☐ Call   ☐ Email   ☐ Text   ☐ Postcard   ☐ Other_____

Discussed:
_____
_____
_____

INDUSTRY CONTACT TRACKER

Agent Connection
Name/ Agency   Date Contacted

_____

Contacted:
☐ Call   ☐ Email   ☐ Text   ☐ Postcard   ☐ Other_____

Following up:
_____
_____
_____

Casting Director Connection
Name/ Company   Date Contacted

_____

Contacted:
☐ Call   ☐ Email   ☐ Text   ☐ Postcard   ☐ Other_____

Following up:
_____
_____
_____

Industry Connection
(Director, Producer, Showrunner, Exec. Assistant, etc.)
Name/ Position/Company   Date Contacted

_____

Contacted:
☐ Call   ☐ Email   ☐ Text   ☐ Postcard   ☐ Other_____

Following up:
_____
_____
_____

INDUSTRY MEETING

Date : _____   Time : _____

Person/Company_____

Address
_____

_____   In Person

_____   On Camera

                             On Zoom

REASON FOR MEETING

NOTES

JANUARY

THREE THINGS YOU'VE ACCOMPLISHED AND/OR PEOPLE YOU'VE MET

THREE LESSONS YOU'VE LEARNED

FEBRUARY

ACTING GOALS

LIFE GOALS

MONTHLY BUDGET

INCOME

INCOME-1	
INCOME-2	
OTHER INCOME	
BUDGET	

EXPENSES

MONTHLY LIVING

ACTING

BILL TO BE PAID	DUE DATE	AMOUNT	PAID	NOTES
_____	_____	_____	_____	
_____	_____	_____	_____	
_____	_____	_____	_____	
_____	_____	_____	_____	
_____	_____	_____	_____	
_____	_____	_____	_____	
_____	_____	_____	_____	
_____	_____	_____	_____	

MONTHLY SUMMARY

TOTAL INCOME	TOTAL EXPENSES	DIFFERENCE

FEBRUARY

M	T	W	T

Notes

 # MONTHLY PLANNER

F	S	S

Acting Priorities

_____
_____
_____
_____
_____
_____
_____
_____

Career Priorities

_____
_____
_____
_____
_____
_____
_____
_____

Life Priorities

_____
_____
_____
_____
_____
_____
_____
_____

Positive Thoughts/Prayers/Affirmations

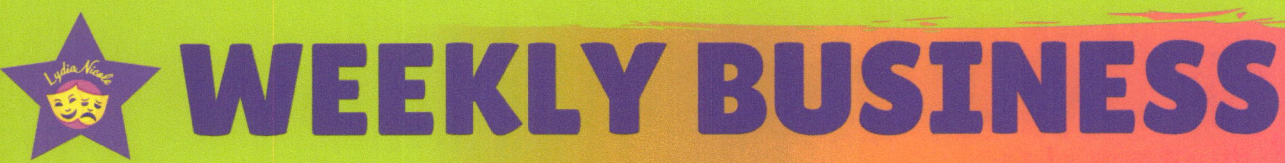

WEEKLY BUSINESS

ACTING　　　　**BOOKINGS**　　　　**PROJECTS**

SUNDAY

MONDAY

TUESDAY

WEDNESDAY

THURSDAY

FRIDAY

SATURDAY

THOUGHTS

WEEKLY BUSINESS

ACTING **BOOKINGS** **PROJECTS**

SUNDAY

MONDAY

TUESDAY

WEDNESDAY

THURSDAY

FRIDAY

SATURDAY

THOUGHTS

WEEKLY BUSINESS

ACTING **BOOKINGS** **PROJECTS**

SUNDAY

MONDAY

TUESDAY

WEDNESDAY

THURSDAY

FRIDAY

SATURDAY

THOUGHTS

WEEKLY BUSINESS

ACTING　　　　**BOOKINGS**　　　　**PROJECTS**

SUNDAY

MONDAY

TUESDAY

WEDNESDAY

THURSDAY

FRIDAY

SATURDAY

THOUGHTS

WHAT TO COMPLETE

LEAVE FOR LATER

AUDITION TRACKER

Date: _____

☐ Self Tape   ☐ Request   ☐ Callback   ☐ Producers

☐ In-Person Audition   ☐ Zoom   ☐ Sides   ☐ Script

Number of callbacks ☐   ☐ Booked it

MY MOOD: ☺️ 🥰 😳 😎 🤔 😜 🤓 😴 😢 🥶 😠 😡

Contact Info

Address

_____

_____

_____

_____

Email

_____

_____

Cell Phone

_____

_____

Wardrobe/Hair/Make-Up

*Include selfie of yourself before audition

_____

_____

_____

_____

Project / Title / Role

_____

_____

Production Company

Director / Writer

Casting

Casting Director

_____

_____

Casting Assoc.

_____

_____

Casting Asst.

AUDITION TRACKER

Date:_____

- ■ Self Tape
- ■ In-Person Audition
- ■ Request
- ■ Zoom
- ■ Callback
- ■ Sides
- ■ Producers
- ■ Script

Number of callbacks [ ]   ■ Booked it

MY MOOD: ☺️ 🥰 🥺 😎 🤔 🤭 🤪 😴 😢 🥶 😡 😠

Contact Info

Address
_____
_____
_____
_____

Email
_____
_____

Cell Phone
_____
_____

Wardrobe/Hair/Make-Up
*Include selfie of yourself before audition
_____
_____
_____
_____

Project / Title / Role
_____
_____

Production Company

Director / Writer

Casting

Casting Director
_____
_____

Casting Assoc.
_____
_____

Casting Asst.
_____

AUDITION TRACKER

Date: _____

☐ Self Tape ☐ Request ☐ Callback ☐ Producers

☐ In-Person Audition ☐ Zoom ☐ Sides ☐ Script

Number of callbacks [   ] ☐ Booked it

MY MOOD: 🤗 🥰 🥺 😎 🤨 😚 🤪 😴 🤕 🥶 😠 😡

Contact Info

Address
_____
_____
_____

Email
_____
_____

Cell Phone
_____
_____

Wardrobe/Hair/Make-Up
*Include selfie of yourself before audition
_____
_____
_____
_____

Project / Title / Role
_____
_____

Production Company

Director / Writer

Casting

Casting Director
_____
_____

Casting Assoc.
_____
_____

Casting Asst.
_____

AGENT/MANAGER TRACKER

Name	Title	Birthday
_____	_____	_____
_____	_____	_____
_____	_____	_____

Address
_____
_____
_____

Cell Phone   Email
_____   _____
_____   _____
_____   _____

Best day and time to contact
_____
_____

Other important information

AGENT/MANAGER TRACKER

DAY CALLED /VISITED	PURPOSE	OUTCOME

MY MOOD:

DAY CALLED /VISITED	PURPOSE	OUTCOME

MY MOOD:

DAY CALLED /VISITED	PURPOSE	OUTCOME

MY MOOD:

DAY CALLED /VISITED	PURPOSE	OUTCOME

MY MOOD:

CALLED INTO SAY UNAVAILABLE	FROM	UNTIL
DATE:	DATE:	DATE:

MY MOOD:

NOTES

INDUSTRY CONTACT TRACKER

Agent Connection
Name/ Agency   Date Contacted

_____

Contacted:
🟩 Call   🟩 Email   🟩 Text   🟩 Postcard   🟩 Other_____

Discussed:
_____
_____
_____

Casting Director Connection
Name/ Company   Date Contacted

_____

Contacted:
🟩 Call   🟩 Email   🟩 Text   🟩 Postcard   🟩 Other_____

Discussed:
_____
_____
_____

Industry Connection
(Director, Producer, Showrunner, Exec. Assistant, etc.)
Name/ Position/Company   Date Contacted

_____

Contacted:
🟩 Call   🟩 Email   🟩 Text   🟩 Postcard   🟩 Other_____

Discussed:
_____
_____
_____

INDUSTRY CONTACT TRACKER

Agent Connection
Name/ Agency   Date Contacted

_____

Contacted:
☐ Call   ☐ Email   ☐ Text   ☐ Postcard   ☐ Other_____

Following up:
_____
_____
_____

Casting Director Connection
Name/ Company   Date Contacted

_____

Contacted:
☐ Call   ☐ Email   ☐ Text   ☐ Postcard   ☐ Other_____

Following up:
_____
_____
_____

Industry Connection
(Director, Producer, Showrunner, Exec. Assistant, etc.)
Name/ Position/Company   Date Contacted

_____

Contacted:
☐ Call   ☐ Email   ☐ Text   ☐ Postcard   ☐ Other_____

Following up:
_____
_____
_____

INDUSTRY MEETING

Date : _____   Time : _____

Person/Company_____

Address
_____

_____   ☐ In Person

_____   ☐ On Camera

                                         ☐ On Zoom

REASON FOR MEETING

NOTES

FEBRUARY

THREE THINGS YOU'VE ACCOMPLISHED AND/OR PEOPLE YOU'VE MET

THREE LESSONS YOU'VE LEARNED

MARCH

ACTING GOALS

LIFE GOALS

MONTHLY BUDGET

INCOME		EXPENSES
INCOME-1		**MONTHLY LIVING**
INCOME-2		
OTHER INCOME		**ACTING**
BUDGET		

BILL TO BE PAID	DUE DATE	AMOUNT	PAID	NOTES
_____	_____	_____	_____	
_____	_____	_____	_____	
_____	_____	_____	_____	
_____	_____	_____	_____	
_____	_____	_____	_____	
_____	_____	_____	_____	
_____	_____	_____	_____	
_____	_____	_____	_____	
_____	_____	_____	_____	
_____	_____	_____	_____	

MONTHLY SUMMARY

TOTAL INCOME	TOTAL EXPENSES	DIFFERENCE

MARCH

M	T	W	T

Notes

MONTHLY PLANNER

F	S	S

Positive Thoughts/Prayers/Affirmations

Acting Priorities

_____
_____
_____
_____
_____
_____
_____
_____

Career Priorities

_____
_____
_____
_____
_____
_____
_____
_____

Life Priorities

_____
_____
_____
_____
_____
_____
_____
_____

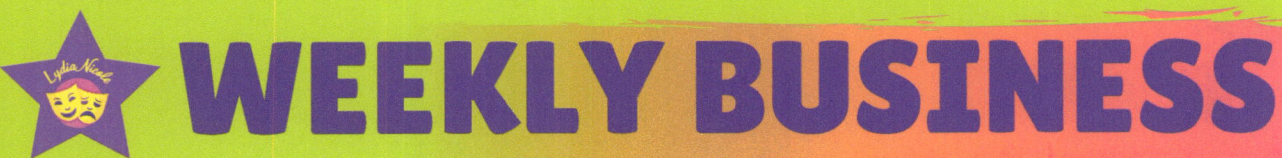

WEEKLY BUSINESS

ACTING	BOOKINGS	PROJECTS

SUNDAY

MONDAY

TUESDAY

WEDNESDAY

THURSDAY

FRIDAY

SATURDAY

THOUGHTS

WEEKLY BUSINESS

ACTING

BOOKINGS

PROJECTS

SUNDAY

MONDAY

TUESDAY

WEDNESDAY

THURSDAY

FRIDAY

SATURDAY

THOUGHTS

WEEKLY BUSINESS

ACTING **BOOKINGS** **PROJECTS**

SUNDAY

MONDAY

TUESDAY

WEDNESDAY

THURSDAY

FRIDAY

SATURDAY

THOUGHTS

WEEKLY BUSINESS

ACTING **BOOKINGS** **PROJECTS**

SUNDAY

MONDAY

TUESDAY

WEDNESDAY

THURSDAY

FRIDAY

SATURDAY

THOUGHTS

WHAT TO COMPLETE

LEAVE FOR LATER

AUDITION TRACKER

Date:_____

- ☐ Self Tape
- ☐ In-Person Audition
- ☐ Request
- ☐ Zoom
- ☐ Callback
- ☐ Sides
- ☐ Producers
- ☐ Script

Number of callbacks ☐   ☐ Booked it

MY MOOD: 😊 🥰 🥺 😎 🤨 🥳 🤪 😴 🥺 🥶 😠 😡

Contact Info

Address
_____
_____
_____
_____

Email
_____
_____

Cell Phone
_____
_____

Wardrobe/Hair/Make-Up
*Include selfie of yourself before audition
_____
_____
_____
_____

Project / Title / Role
_____
_____

Production Company

Director / Writer

Casting

Casting Director
_____
_____

Casting Assoc.
_____
_____

Casting Asst.
_____

AUDITION TRACKER

Date:_____

- ☐ Self Tape
- ☐ In-Person Audition
- ☐ Request
- ☐ Zoom
- ☐ Callback
- ☐ Sides
- ☐ Producers
- ☐ Script

Number of callbacks ☐   ☐ Booked it

MY MOOD: 🙂 🥰 🥺 😎 🤔 😳 🤪 😴 😢 🥶 😡 😠

Contact Info

Address
_____
_____
_____
_____

Email
_____
_____
_____

Cell Phone
_____
_____

Wardrobe/Hair/Make-Up
_____
*Include selfie of yourself before audition
_____
_____
_____
_____

Project / Title / Role
_____
_____

Production Company

Director / Writer

Casting

Casting Director
_____

Casting Assoc.
_____

Casting Asst.

AUDITION TRACKER

Date:_____

- ☐ Self Tape
- ☐ In-Person Audition
- ☐ Request
- ☐ Zoom
- ☐ Callback
- ☐ Sides
- ☐ Producers
- ☐ Script

Number of callbacks ☐   ☐ Booked it

MY MOOD: ☺️ 🥰 🥺 😎 🤔 🤭 🤪 😴 🥹 🥶 😠 😡

Contact Info

Address
_____
_____
_____

Email
_____
_____

Cell Phone
_____
_____

Wardrobe/Hair/Make-Up
*Include selfie of yourself before audition

_____
_____
_____
_____

Project / Title / Role
_____
_____

Production Company

Director / Writer

Casting

Casting Director
_____
_____

Casting Assoc.
_____
_____

Casting Asst.
_____

AGENT/MANAGER TRACKER

Name	Title	Birthday
_____	_____	_____
_____	_____	_____
_____	_____	_____

Address
_____
_____
_____

Cell Phone
_____
_____
_____

Email
_____
_____
_____

Best day and time to contact
_____
_____

Other important information

AGENT/MANAGER TRACKER

DAY CALLED /VISITED	PURPOSE	OUTCOME	NOTES

MY MOOD:

DAY CALLED /VISITED	PURPOSE	OUTCOME

MY MOOD:

DAY CALLED /VISITED	PURPOSE	OUTCOME

MY MOOD:

DAY CALLED /VISITED	PURPOSE	OUTCOME

MY MOOD:

CALLED INTO SAY UNAVAILABLE	FROM	UNTIL
DATE:	DATE:	DATE:

MY MOOD:

INDUSTRY CONTACT TRACKER

Agent Connection

Name/ Agency   Date Contacted

_____

Contacted:

🟩 Call   🟩 Email   🟩 Text   🟩 Postcard   🟩 Other_____

Discussed:
_____
_____
_____

Casting Director Connection

Name/ Company   Date Contacted

_____

Contacted:

🟩 Call   🟩 Email   🟩 Text   🟩 Postcard   🟩 Other_____

Discussed:
_____
_____
_____

Industry Connection
(Director, Producer, Showrunner, Exec. Assistant, etc.)
Name/ Position/Company   Date Contacted

_____

Contacted:

🟩 Call   🟩 Email   🟩 Text   🟩 Postcard   🟩 Other_____

Discussed:
_____
_____
_____

INDUSTRY CONTACT TRACKER

Agent Connection
Name/ Agency   Date Contacted

_____

Contacted:
☐ Call   ☐ Email   ☐ Text   ☐ Postcard   ☐ Other_____

Following up:
_____
_____
_____

Casting Director Connection
Name/ Company   Date Contacted

_____

Contacted:
☐ Call   ☐ Email   ☐ Text   ☐ Postcard   ☐ Other_____

Following up:
_____
_____
_____

Industry Connection
(Director, Producer, Showrunner, Exec. Assistant, etc.)
Name/ Position/Company   Date Contacted

_____

Contacted:
☐ Call   ☐ Email   ☐ Text   ☐ Postcard   ☐ Other_____

Following up:
_____
_____
_____

INDUSTRY MEETING

Date : _____   Time : _____

Person/Company_____

Address
_____

_____   ☐ In Person

_____   ☐ On Camera

                                                   ☐ On Zoom

REASON FOR MEETING

NOTES

MARCH

THREE THINGS YOU'VE ACCOMPLISHED AND/OR PEOPLE YOU'VE MET

THREE LESSONS YOU'VE LEARNED

APRIL

ACTING GOALS

LIFE GOALS

MONTHLY BUDGET

INCOME

INCOME-1	
INCOME-2	
OTHER INCOME	
BUDGET	

EXPENSES

MONTHLY LIVING

ACTING

BILL TO BE PAID	DUE DATE	AMOUNT	PAID	NOTES
_____	_____	_____	_____	
_____	_____	_____	_____	
_____	_____	_____	_____	
_____	_____	_____	_____	
_____	_____	_____	_____	
_____	_____	_____	_____	
_____	_____	_____	_____	
_____	_____	_____	_____	
_____	_____	_____	_____	

MONTHLY SUMMARY

TOTAL INCOME	TOTAL EXPENSES	DIFFERENCE

APRIL

M	T	W	T

Notes

MONTHLY PLANNER

F	S	S

Positive Thoughts/Prayers/Affirmations

Acting Priorities

_____
_____
_____
_____
_____
_____
_____
_____
_____

Career Priorities

_____
_____
_____
_____
_____
_____
_____
_____

Life Priorities

_____
_____
_____
_____
_____
_____
_____

WEEKLY BUSINESS

ACTING **BOOKINGS** **PROJECTS**

SUNDAY

MONDAY

TUESDAY

WEDNESDAY

THURSDAY

FRIDAY

SATURDAY

THOUGHTS

WEEKLY BUSINESS

ACTING   **BOOKINGS**   **PROJECTS**

SUNDAY

MONDAY

TUESDAY

WEDNESDAY

THURSDAY

FRIDAY

SATURDAY

THOUGHTS

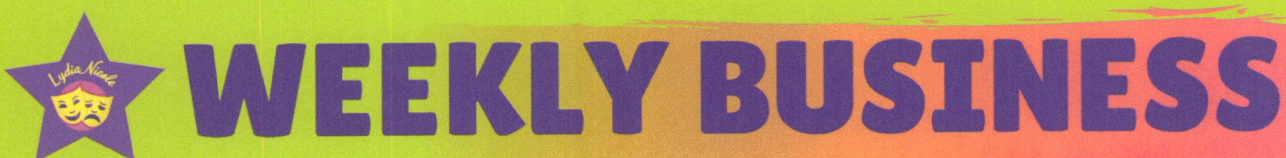

WEEKLY BUSINESS

ACTING **BOOKINGS** **PROJECTS**

SUNDAY

MONDAY

TUESDAY

WEDNESDAY

THURSDAY

FRIDAY

SATURDAY

THOUGHTS

WEEKLY BUSINESS

ACTING **BOOKINGS** **PROJECTS**

SUNDAY

MONDAY

TUESDAY

WEDNESDAY

THURSDAY

FRIDAY

SATURDAY

THOUGHTS

WHAT TO COMPLETE

LEAVE FOR LATER

AUDITION TRACKER

Date:_____

- ☐ Self Tape
- ☐ Request
- ☐ Callback
- ☐ Producers
- ☐ In-Person Audition
- ☐ Zoom
- ☐ Sides
- ☐ Script

Number of callbacks ☐   ☐ Booked it

MY MOOD: ☺️ 🥰 🥺 😎 🤨 🥴 🤪 😴 🥺 🥶 😡 😠

Contact Info

Address
_____
_____
_____
_____

Email
_____
_____

Cell Phone
_____
_____

Wardrobe/Hair/Make-Up
*Include selfie of yourself before audition

_____
_____
_____
_____

Project / Title / Role
_____
_____

Production Company

Director / Writer

Casting

Casting Director
_____
_____

Casting Assoc.
_____
_____

Casting Asst.

AUDITION TRACKER

Date:_____

- ☐ Self Tape
- ☐ In-Person Audition
- ☐ Request
- ☐ Zoom
- ☐ Callback
- ☐ Sides
- ☐ Producers
- ☐ Script

Number of callbacks ☐   ☐ Booked it

MY MOOD: 😊 🥰 🥺 😎 🤨 🥳 🤓 😴 🥶 🥵 😡

Contact Info

Address
_____
_____
_____
_____

Email
_____
_____
_____

Cell Phone
_____
_____

Wardrobe/Hair/Make-Up
_____
*Include selfie of yourself before audition

_____
_____
_____
_____

Project / Title / Role
_____
_____

Production Company

Director / Writer

Casting

Casting Director
_____

Casting Assoc.
_____

Casting Asst.
_____

AUDITION TRACKER

Date:_____

- ☐ Self Tape
- ☐ In-Person Audition
- ☐ Request
- ☐ Zoom
- ☐ Callback
- ☐ Sides
- ☐ Producers
- ☐ Script

Number of callbacks ☐   ☐ Booked it

MY MOOD: 🥰 😍 🥺 😎 🤔 🤭 🤪 😴 🥹 🥶 😠 🤬

Contact Info

Address
_____
_____
_____
_____

Email
_____
_____

Cell Phone
_____
_____

Wardrobe/Hair/Make-Up
_____
*Include selfie of yourself before audition
_____
_____
_____
_____

Project / Title / Role
_____
_____

Production Company

Director / Writer

Casting

Casting Director
_____
_____

Casting Assoc.
_____
_____

Casting Asst.

AGENT/MANAGER TRACKER

Name	Title	Birthday
_____	_____	_____
_____	_____	_____
_____	_____	_____

Address
_____
_____
_____

Cell Phone   Email
_____   _____
_____   _____
_____

Best day and time to contact
_____
_____

Other important information

AGENT/MANAGER TRACKER

DAY CALLED /VISITED	PURPOSE	OUTCOME

MY MOOD:

DAY CALLED /VISITED	PURPOSE	OUTCOME

MY MOOD:

DAY CALLED /VISITED	PURPOSE	OUTCOME

MY MOOD:

DAY CALLED /VISITED	PURPOSE	OUTCOME

MY MOOD:

CALLED INTO SAY UNAVAILABLE	FROM	UNTIL
DATE:	DATE:	DATE:

MY MOOD:

NOTES

INDUSTRY CONTACT TRACKER

Agent Connection

Name/ Agency   Date Contacted

_____

Contacted:

☐ Call   ☐ Email   ☐ Text   ☐ Postcard   ☐ Other_____

Discussed:

_____

_____

_____

Casting Director Connection

Name/ Company   Date Contacted

_____

Contacted:

☐ Call   ☐ Email   ☐ Text   ☐ Postcard   ☐ Other_____

Discussed:

_____

_____

_____

Industry Connection

(Director, Producer, Showrunner, Exec. Assistant, etc.)

Name/ Position/Company   Date Contacted

_____

Contacted:

☐ Call   ☐ Email   ☐ Text   ☐ Postcard   ☐ Other_____

Discussed:

_____

_____

_____

INDUSTRY CONTACT TRACKER

Agent Connection
Name/ Agency   Date Contacted

_____

Contacted:
☐ Call   ☐ Email   ☐ Text   ☐ Postcard   ☐ Other_____

Following up:
_____
_____
_____

Casting Director Connection
Name/ Company   Date Contacted

_____

Contacted:
☐ Call   ☐ Email   ☐ Text   ☐ Postcard   ☐ Other_____

Following up:
_____
_____
_____

Industry Connection
(Director, Producer, Showrunner, Exec. Assistant, etc.)
Name/ Position/Company   Date Contacted

_____

Contacted:
☐ Call   ☐ Email   ☐ Text   ☐ Postcard   ☐ Other_____

Following up:
_____
_____
_____

INDUSTRY MEETING

Date : _____   Time : _____

Person/Company_____

Address

_____

_____   ☐ In Person

_____   ☐ On Camera

                                        ☐ On Zoom

REASON FOR MEETING

NOTES

APRIL

THREE THINGS YOU'VE ACCOMPLISHED AND/OR PEOPLE YOU'VE MET

THREE LESSONS YOU'VE LEARNED

MAY

ACTING GOALS

LIFE GOALS

MONTHLY BUDGET

INCOME

INCOME-1	
INCOME-2	
OTHER INCOME	
BUDGET	

EXPENSES

MONTHLY LIVING

ACTING

BILL TO BE PAID	DUE DATE	AMOUNT	PAID	NOTES
_____	_____	_____	_____	
_____	_____	_____	_____	
_____	_____	_____	_____	
_____	_____	_____	_____	
_____	_____	_____	_____	
_____	_____	_____	_____	
_____	_____	_____	_____	
_____	_____	_____	_____	
_____	_____	_____	_____	

MONTHLY SUMMARY

TOTAL INCOME	TOTAL EXPENSES	DIFFERENCE

 # MAY

M	T	W	T

Notes

MONTHLY PLANNER

F	S	S

Positive Thoughts/Prayers/Affirmations

Acting Priorities

_____
_____
_____
_____
_____
_____
_____
_____
_____

Career Priorities

_____
_____
_____
_____
_____
_____
_____
_____

Life Priorities

_____
_____
_____
_____
_____
_____
_____
_____

WEEKLY BUSINESS

ACTING   **BOOKINGS**   **PROJECTS**

SUNDAY

MONDAY

TUESDAY

WEDNESDAY

THURSDAY

FRIDAY

SATURDAY

THOUGHTS

WEEKLY BUSINESS

ACTING **BOOKINGS** **PROJECTS**

SUNDAY

MONDAY

TUESDAY

WEDNESDAY

THURSDAY

FRIDAY

SATURDAY

THOUGHTS

WEEKLY BUSINESS

ACTING

BOOKINGS

PROJECTS

SUNDAY

MONDAY

TUESDAY

WEDNESDAY

THURSDAY

FRIDAY

SATURDAY

THOUGHTS

WEEKLY BUSINESS

ACTING

BOOKINGS

PROJECTS

SUNDAY

MONDAY

TUESDAY

WEDNESDAY

THURSDAY

FRIDAY

SATURDAY

THOUGHTS

WHAT TO COMPLETE

LEAVE FOR LATER

AUDITION TRACKER

Date:_____

- ☑ Self Tape
- ☑ In-Person Audition
- ☑ Request
- ☑ Zoom
- ☑ Callback
- ☑ Sides
- ☑ Producers
- ☑ Script

Number of callbacks ⬜   ☑ Booked it

MY MOOD: 😌 🥰 🙄 😎 🤔 🥲 🤪 😴 🥺 😬 😠 😡

Contact Info

Address
_____
_____
_____

Email
_____
_____

Cell Phone
_____
_____

Wardrobe/Hair/Make-Up
*Include selfie of yourself before audition
_____
_____
_____
_____

Project / Title / Role

_____
_____

Production Company

Director / Writer

Casting

Casting Director
_____
_____

Casting Assoc.
_____
_____

Casting Asst.
_____

AUDITION TRACKER

Date:_____

- ☐ Self Tape
- ☐ In-Person Audition
- ☐ Request
- ☐ Zoom
- ☐ Callback
- ☐ Sides
- ☐ Producers
- ☐ Script

Number of callbacks ☐

☐ Booked it

MY MOOD: 😌 🥰 🙄 😎 🤔 😊 🤪 😴 😢 🥶 😡 😠

Contact Info

Address _____

_____

_____

_____

Email _____

_____

_____

Cell Phone _____

_____

_____

Wardrobe/Hair/Make-Up

*Include selfie of yourself before audition

_____

_____

_____

_____

Project / Title / Role

_____

_____

Production Company

Director / Writer

Casting

Casting Director

_____

Casting Assoc.

_____

Casting Asst.

AUDITION TRACKER

Date: _____

- ☐ Self Tape
- ☐ In-Person Audition
- ☐ Request
- ☐ Zoom
- ☐ Callback
- ☐ Sides
- ☐ Producers
- ☐ Script

Number of callbacks ☐ ☐ Booked it

MY MOOD: 🙂 🥰 😳 😎 🤔 🥲 🤪 😴 😢 😬 😠 😡

Contact Info

Address _____

_____

_____

_____

Email _____

_____

_____

Cell Phone _____

_____

Wardrobe/Hair/Make-Up _____

*Include selfie of yourself before audition

_____

_____

_____

_____

Project / Title / Role

_____

_____

Production Company

Director / Writer

Casting

Casting Director

_____

Casting Assoc.

_____

Casting Asst.

_____

AGENT/MANAGER TRACKER

Name **Title** **Birthday**

_____ _____ _____

_____ _____ _____

_____ _____ _____

Address
_____

_____

_____

Cell Phone   Email

_____   _____

_____   _____

_____   _____

Best day and time to contact
_____

_____

Other important information

AGENT/MANAGER TRACKER

DAY CALLED /VISITED	PURPOSE	OUTCOME	NOTES

MY MOOD:

DAY CALLED /VISITED	PURPOSE	OUTCOME

MY MOOD:

DAY CALLED /VISITED	PURPOSE	OUTCOME

MY MOOD:

DAY CALLED /VISITED	PURPOSE	OUTCOME

MY MOOD:

CALLED INTO SAY UNAVAILABLE	FROM	UNTIL
DATE:	DATE:	DATE:

MY MOOD:

INDUSTRY CONTACT TRACKER

Agent Connection
Name/ Agency   Date Contacted
_____

Contacted:
■ Call   ■ Email   ■ Text   ■ Postcard   ■ Other_____

Discussed:
_____
_____
_____

Casting Director Connection
Name/ Company   Date Contacted
_____

Contacted:
■ Call   ■ Email   ■ Text   ■ Postcard   ■ Other_____

Discussed:
_____
_____
_____

Industry Connection
(Director, Producer, Showrunner, Exec. Assistant, etc.)
Name/ Position/Company   Date Contacted
_____

Contacted:
■ Call   ■ Email   ■ Text   ■ Postcard   ■ Other_____

Discussed:
_____
_____
_____

INDUSTRY CONTACT TRACKER

Agent Connection
Name/ Agency   Date Contacted

_____

Contacted:
- ☐ Call
- ☐ Email
- ☐ Text
- ☐ Postcard
- ☐ Other_____

Following up:

_____

_____

_____

Casting Director Connection
Name/ Company   Date Contacted

_____

Contacted:
- ☐ Call
- ☐ Email
- ☐ Text
- ☐ Postcard
- ☐ Other_____

Following up:

_____

_____

_____

Industry Connection
(Director, Producer, Showrunner, Exec. Assistant, etc.)
Name/ Position/Company   Date Contacted

_____

Contacted:
- ☐ Call
- ☐ Email
- ☐ Text
- ☐ Postcard
- ☐ Other_____

Following up:

_____

_____

_____

INDUSTRY MEETING

Date : _____   Time : _____

Person/Company _____

Address
_____   ☐ In Person

_____   ☐ On Camera

_____   ☐ On Zoom

REASON FOR MEETING

NOTES

MAY

THREE THINGS YOU'VE ACCOMPLISHED AND/OR PEOPLE YOU'VE MET

THREE LESSONS YOU'VE LEARNED

PRODUCTIVITY *Challenge*

REVIEW YOUR ACTING WORK	WHAT KIND OF ACTOR DO YOU WANT TO BE	DISCOVER WHAT YOU SELL	PICK A MONOLOGUE THAT IS ON BRAND FOR YOU	AUDIT AN ACTING CLASS
TRY OUT A NEW GYM	LEARN NEW BREATHING TECHNIQUE	READ A CLASSIC PLAY	CHECK IN WITH YOUR AGENT	GET INTO AN ACTORS MASTER MIND GROUP
RESEARCH COMPETITORS HEADSHOTS	REVIEW YOUR HEADSHOTS	SELECT A PHOTOGRAPHER	SUBMIT FOR ACTING ROLES	REVIEW YOUR FINANCIAL BUDGET
UPDATE YOUR SOCIAL MEDIA PROFILES	MAKE A DIRECTOR TARGET LIST	CREATE /UPDATE YOUR WEBSITE	UPDATE YOUR RESUME	LEARN ABOUT YOUR FAVORITE ACTORS
PRACTICE TIME MANAGEMENT	MAKE A DIRECTOR TARGET LIST	UPDATE YOUR IMDBPRO	LEARN A NEW SKILL FOR ACTING	USE POMODORO TECHNIQUE
READ AN ACTING BOOK	TAKE A STRETCH CLASS	LEARN ABOUT UNION PERKS	FIND TWO AUDITION PARTNERS	MAKE A TV SHOW TARGET LIST

30 DAY
SELF-LOVE CHALLENGE

SOCIAL MEDIA DAY FAST	THROW AWAY SOMETHING OLD & WORN	LISTEN TO AN INSPIRING PODCAST	COMPLIMENT A STRANGER	SCHEDULE A GAME NIGHT
GET A MASSAGE	TAKE A RIDE TO THE BEACH	MAKE A NOT FOR ME LIST	READ A BOOK FOR 15 MINUTES	START A HOBBY
GO FOR A WALK	TREAT YOURSELF TO SOMETHING FABULOUS	HAVE COFFEE WITH A FRIEND	LEARN A NEW SKILL	WALK IN NATURE
DO A SPA DAY	HAVE A PLAY DATE	TAKE A GOOD NAP	ORGANIZE YOUR CLOSET	TAKE A DETOX BATH
DO 20 MINUTES OF YOGA	BE OF SERVICE TO SOMEONE	GO ON AN ARTIST DATE	MAKE A BUCKET LIST	MEDITATE
CREATE AN UPLIFTING MUSIC PLAYLIST	WATCH THE SUNRISE	START LEARNING A NEW LANGUAGE	READ 15 MINUTES OF A HOLY BOOK	CREATE A SELF-CARE KIT

JUNE

ACTING GOALS

LIFE GOALS

MONTHLY BUDGET

INCOME

INCOME-1	
OTHER INCOME	
INCOME-2	
BUDGET	

EXPENSES

MONTHLY LIVING

ACTING

BILL TO BE PAID	DUE DATE	AMOUNT	PAID	NOTES

MONTHLY SUMMARY

TOTAL INCOME	TOTAL EXPENSES	DIFFERENCE

JUNE

M	T	W	T

Notes

 # MONTHLY PLANNER

F	S	S

Positive Thoughts/Prayers/Affirmations

Acting Priorities
_____
_____
_____
_____
_____
_____
_____
_____

Career Priorities
_____
_____
_____
_____
_____
_____
_____
_____

Life Priorities
_____
_____
_____
_____
_____
_____
_____
_____

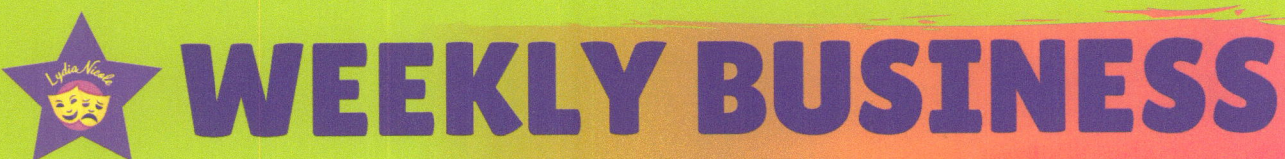

WEEKLY BUSINESS

ACTING **BOOKINGS** **PROJECTS**

SUNDAY

MONDAY

TUESDAY

WEDNESDAY

THURSDAY

FRIDAY

SATURDAY

THOUGHTS

WEEKLY BUSINESS

ACTING **BOOKINGS** **PROJECTS**

SUNDAY

MONDAY

TUESDAY

WEDNESDAY

THURSDAY

FRIDAY

SATURDAY

THOUGHTS

WEEKLY BUSINESS

ACTING   **BOOKINGS**   **PROJECTS**

SUNDAY

MONDAY

TUESDAY

WEDNESDAY

THURSDAY

FRIDAY

SATURDAY

THOUGHTS

WEEKLY BUSINESS

ACTING   **BOOKINGS**   **PROJECTS**

SUNDAY

MONDAY

TUESDAY

WEDNESDAY

THURSDAY

FRIDAY

SATURDAY

THOUGHTS

WHAT TO COMPLETE

LEAVE FOR LATER

AUDITION TRACKER

Date:_____

- ☐ Self Tape
- ☐ In-Person Audition
- ☐ Request
- ☐ Zoom
- ☐ Callback
- ☐ Sides
- ☐ Producers
- ☐ Script

Number of callbacks ☐   ☐ Booked it

MY MOOD: 🙂 🥰 🥺 😎 🤔 😚 🤪 😴 🥶 🤢 😡 🤬

Contact Info

Address
_____
_____
_____

Email
_____
_____

Cell Phone
_____

Wardrobe/Hair/Make-Up
*Include selfie of yourself before audition
_____
_____
_____
_____

Project / Title / Role
_____
_____

Production Company

Director / Writer

Casting

Casting Director
_____

Casting Assoc.
_____

Casting Asst.

AUDITION TRACKER

Date:_____

☐ **Self Tape** ☐ **Request** ☐ **Callback** ☐ **Producers**

☐ **In-Person Audition** ☐ **Zoom** ☐ **Sides** ☐ **Script**

Number of callbacks [ ] ☐ **Booked it**

MY MOOD: ☺ 🥰 👀 😎 🤔 🥰 🤪 😴 🥲 🥶 😠 😡

Contact Info

Address

_____

_____

_____

Email

_____

_____

Cell Phone

_____

_____

Wardrobe/Hair/Make-Up

*Include selfie of yourself before audition

_____

_____

_____

_____

Project / Title / Role

_____

_____

Production Company

Director / Writer

Casting

Casting Director

_____

_____

Casting Assoc.

_____

_____

Casting Asst.

_____

AUDITION TRACKER

Date:_____

- ■ Self Tape
- ■ In-Person Audition
- ■ Request
- ■ Zoom
- ■ Callback
- ■ Sides
- ■ Producers
- ■ Script

Number of callbacks ☐   ■ Booked it

MY MOOD: 🙂 🥰 🥺 😎 🤔 🤭 🤪 😴 🥶 🥶 😠 😡

Contact Info

Address _____

_____

_____

_____

Email _____

_____

_____

Cell Phone _____

_____

Wardrobe/Hair/Make-Up
*Include selfie of yourself before audition

_____

_____

_____

_____

Project / Title / Role

_____

_____

Production Company

Director / Writer

Casting

Casting Director
_____

_____

Casting Assoc.
_____

_____

Casting Asst.

AGENT/MANAGER TRACKER

Name	Title	Birthday
_____	_____	_____
_____	_____	_____
_____	_____	_____

Address
_____
_____
_____

Cell Phone	Email
_____	_____
_____	_____

Best day and time to contact
_____
_____

Other important information

AGENT/MANAGER TRACKER

DAY CALLED /VISITED	PURPOSE	OUTCOME	NOTES

MY MOOD:

DAY CALLED /VISITED	PURPOSE	OUTCOME

MY MOOD:

DAY CALLED /VISITED	PURPOSE	OUTCOME

MY MOOD:

DAY CALLED /VISITED	PURPOSE	OUTCOME

MY MOOD:

CALLED INTO SAY UNAVAILABLE	FROM	UNTIL
DATE:	DATE:	DATE:

MY MOOD:

INDUSTRY CONTACT TRACKER

Agent Connection

Name/ Agency   Date Contacted

_____

Contacted:
- ☐ Call   ☐ Email   ☐ Text   ☐ Postcard   ☐ Other_____

Discussed:
_____
_____
_____

Casting Director Connection

Name/ Company   Date Contacted

_____

Contacted:
- ☐ Call   ☐ Email   ☐ Text   ☐ Postcard   ☐ Other_____

Discussed:
_____
_____
_____

Industry Connection
(Director, Producer, Showrunner, Exec. Assistant, etc.)
Name/ Position/Company   Date Contacted

_____

Contacted:
- ☐ Call   ☐ Email   ☐ Text   ☐ Postcard   ☐ Other_____

Discussed:
_____
_____
_____

INDUSTRY CONTACT TRACKER

Agent Connection
Name/ Agency   Date Contacted

_____

Contacted:
☐ Call   ☐ Email   ☐ Text   ☐ Postcard   ☐ Other_____

Following up:
_____
_____
_____

Casting Director Connection
Name/ Company   Date Contacted

_____

Contacted:
☐ Call   ☐ Email   ☐ Text   ☐ Postcard   ☐ Other_____

Following up:
_____
_____
_____

Industry Connection
(Director, Producer, Showrunner, Exec. Assistant, etc.)
Name/ Position/Company   Date Contacted

_____

Contacted:
☐ Call   ☐ Email   ☐ Text   ☐ Postcard   ☐ Other_____

Following up:
_____
_____
_____

INDUSTRY MEETING

Date : _____   Time : _____

Person/Company_____

Address

_____

_____   ☐ In Person

_____   ☐ On Camera

                                        ☐ On Zoom

REASON FOR MEETING

NOTES

JUNE

THREE THINGS YOU'VE ACCOMPLISHED AND/OR PEOPLE YOU'VE MET

THREE LESSONS YOU'VE LEARNED

JULY

ACTING GOALS

LIFE GOALS

MONTHLY BUDGET

INCOME	
INCOME-1	
INCOME-2	
OTHER INCOME	
BUDGET	

EXPENSES
MONTHLY LIVING
ACTING

BILL TO BE PAID	DUE DATE	AMOUNT	PAID	NOTES
_____	_____	_____	_____	
_____	_____	_____	_____	
_____	_____	_____	_____	
_____	_____	_____	_____	
_____	_____	_____	_____	
_____	_____	_____	_____	
_____	_____	_____	_____	
_____	_____	_____	_____	
_____	_____	_____	_____	

MONTHLY SUMMARY

TOTAL INCOME	TOTAL EXPENSES	DIFFERENCE

JULY

M	T	W	T

Notes

MONTHLY PLANNER

F	S	S

Acting Priorities

_____
_____
_____
_____
_____
_____
_____
_____

Career Priorities

_____
_____
_____
_____
_____
_____
_____
_____

Life Priorities

_____
_____
_____
_____
_____
_____
_____
_____

Positive Thoughts/Prayers/Affirmations

WEEKLY BUSINESS

ACTING

BOOKINGS

PROJECTS

SUNDAY

MONDAY

TUESDAY

WEDNESDAY

THURSDAY

FRIDAY

SATURDAY

THOUGHTS

WEEKLY BUSINESS

ACTING **BOOKINGS** **PROJECTS**

SUNDAY

MONDAY

TUESDAY

WEDNESDAY

THURSDAY

FRIDAY

SATURDAY

THOUGHTS

WEEKLY BUSINESS

ACTING **BOOKINGS** **PROJECTS**

SUNDAY

MONDAY

TUESDAY

WEDNESDAY

THURSDAY

FRIDAY

SATURDAY

THOUGHTS

WEEKLY BUSINESS

ACTING **BOOKINGS** **PROJECTS**

SUNDAY

MONDAY

TUESDAY

WEDNESDAY

THURSDAY

FRIDAY

SATURDAY

THOUGHTS

WHAT TO COMPLETE

LEAVE FOR LATER

AUDITION TRACKER

Date:_____

- ☐ Self Tape
- ☐ In-Person Audition
- ☐ Request
- ☐ Zoom
- ☐ Callback
- ☐ Sides
- ☐ Producers
- ☐ Script

Number of callbacks ☐   ☐ Booked it

MY MOOD: 🙂 🥰 🙄 😎 🤔 🤭 🤪 😴 😢 😬 😠 😡

Contact Info

Address
_____
_____
_____

Email
_____
_____

Cell Phone
_____
_____

Wardrobe/Hair/Make-Up
*Include selfie of yourself before audition
_____
_____
_____
_____

Project / Title / Role
_____
_____

Production Company

Director / Writer

Casting

Casting Director
_____
_____

Casting Assoc.
_____
_____

Casting Asst.

AUDITION TRACKER

Date:_____

- 🟩 Self Tape
- 🟩 In-Person Audition
- 🟩 Request
- 🟩 Zoom
- 🟩 Callback
- 🟩 Sides
- 🟩 Producers
- 🟩 Script

Number of callbacks ⬜   🟩 Booked it

MY MOOD: 😌 🥰 🙄 😎 🤔 🤭 🤪 😴 🥹 🥶 😡 😠

Contact Info

Address
_____
_____
_____

Email
_____
_____

Cell Phone
_____
_____

Wardrobe/Hair/Make-Up
*Include selfie of yourself before audition
_____
_____
_____
_____

Project / Title / Role
_____
_____

Production Company

Director / Writer

Casting

Casting Director
_____

Casting Assoc.
_____

Casting Asst.
_____

AUDITION TRACKER

Date:_____

- ☐ Self Tape
- ☐ In-Person Audition
- ☐ Request
- ☐ Zoom
- ☐ Callback
- ☐ Sides
- ☐ Producers
- ☐ Script

Number of callbacks ☐   ☐ Booked it

MY MOOD: 🙂 🥰 🥺 😎 🤔 🥰 🤪 😴 🥺 🥶 😠 😡

Contact Info

Address
_____
_____
_____
_____

Email
_____
_____
_____

Cell Phone
_____
_____

Wardrobe/Hair/Make-Up
*Include selfie of yourself before audition
_____
_____
_____
_____

Project / Title / Role
_____
_____

Production Company

Director / Writer

Casting

Casting Director
_____
_____

Casting Assoc.
_____
_____

Casting Asst.

AGENT/MANAGER TRACKER

Name	Title	Birthday
_____	_____	_____
_____	_____	_____
_____	_____	_____

Address

_____

_____

_____

Cell Phone

_____

_____

_____

Email

_____

_____

Best day and time to contact

_____

_____

Other important information

AGENT/MANAGER TRACKER

DAY CALLED /VISITED	PURPOSE	OUTCOME	NOTES

MY MOOD:

DAY CALLED /VISITED	PURPOSE	OUTCOME

MY MOOD:

DAY CALLED /VISITED	PURPOSE	OUTCOME

MY MOOD:

DAY CALLED /VISITED	PURPOSE	OUTCOME

MY MOOD:

CALLED INTO SAY UNAVAILABLE	FROM	UNTIL
DATE:	DATE:	DATE:

MY MOOD:

INDUSTRY CONTACT TRACKER

Agent Connection
Name/ Agency   Date Contacted

_____

Contacted:
🟩 Call   🟩 Email   🟩 Text   🟩 Postcard   🟩 Other_____

Discussed:
_____
_____
_____

Casting Director Connection
Name/ Company   Date Contacted

_____

Contacted:
🟩 Call   🟩 Email   🟩 Text   🟩 Postcard   🟩 Other_____

Discussed:
_____
_____
_____

Industry Connection
(Director, Producer, Showrunner, Exec. Assistant, etc.)
Name/ Position/Company   Date Contacted

_____

Contacted:
🟩 Call   🟩 Email   🟩 Text   🟩 Postcard   🟩 Other_____

Discussed:
_____
_____
_____

INDUSTRY CONTACT TRACKER

Agent Connection
Name/ Agency   Date Contacted

_____

Contacted:
☐ Call   ☐ Email   ☐ Text   ☐ Postcard   ☐ Other_____

Following up:
_____
_____
_____

Casting Director Connection
Name/ Company   Date Contacted

_____

Contacted:
☐ Call   ☐ Email   ☐ Text   ☐ Postcard   ☐ Other_____

Following up:
_____
_____
_____

Industry Connection
(Director, Producer, Showrunner, Exec. Assistant, etc.)
Name/ Position/Company   Date Contacted

_____

Contacted:
☐ Call   ☐ Email   ☐ Text   ☐ Postcard   ☐ Other_____

Following up:
_____
_____
_____

INDUSTRY MEETING

Date : _____   Time : _____

Person/Company_____

Address
_____

_____   In Person

_____   On Camera

                                          On Zoom

REASON FOR MEETING

NOTES

JULY

THREE THINGS YOU'VE ACCOMPLISHED AND/OR PEOPLE YOU'VE MET

THREE LESSONS YOU'VE LEARNED

AUGUST

ACTING GOALS

LIFE GOALS

MONTHLY BUDGET

INCOME	
INCOME-1	
INCOME-2	
OTHER INCOME	
BUDGET	

EXPENSES
MONTHLY LIVING
ACTING

BILL TO BE PAID	DUE DATE	AMOUNT	PAID	NOTES
_____	_____	_____	_____	
_____	_____	_____	_____	
_____	_____	_____	_____	
_____	_____	_____	_____	
_____	_____	_____	_____	
_____	_____	_____	_____	
_____	_____	_____	_____	
_____	_____	_____	_____	

MONTHLY SUMMARY

TOTAL INCOME	TOTAL EXPENSES	DIFFERENCE

AUGUST

M	T	W	T

Notes

 # MONTHLY PLANNER

F	S	S

Acting Priorities

_____
_____
_____
_____
_____
_____
_____

Career Priorities

_____
_____
_____
_____
_____
_____
_____

Life Priorities

_____
_____
_____
_____
_____
_____
_____

Positive Thoughts/Prayers/Affirmations

WEEKLY BUSINESS

ACTING　　　　**BOOKINGS**　　　　**PROJECTS**

SUNDAY

MONDAY

TUESDAY

WEDNESDAY

THURSDAY

FRIDAY

SATURDAY

THOUGHTS

WEEKLY BUSINESS

ACTING **BOOKINGS** **PROJECTS**

SUNDAY		THURSDAY	
MONDAY		FRIDAY	
TUESDAY		SATURDAY	
WEDNESDAY		THOUGHTS	

WEEKLY BUSINESS

ACTING　　　　　**BOOKINGS**　　　　　**PROJECTS**

SUNDAY

MONDAY

TUESDAY

WEDNESDAY

THURSDAY

FRIDAY

SATURDAY

THOUGHTS

WEEKLY BUSINESS

ACTING

BOOKINGS

PROJECTS

SUNDAY

MONDAY

TUESDAY

WEDNESDAY

THURSDAY

FRIDAY

SATURDAY

THOUGHTS

WHAT TO COMPLETE

LEAVE FOR LATER

AUDITION TRACKER

Date:_____

- ☐ Self Tape
- ☐ In-Person Audition
- ☐ Request
- ☐ Zoom
- ☐ Callback
- ☐ Sides
- ☐ Producers
- ☐ Script

Number of callbacks ☐   ☐ Booked it

MY MOOD: 🤗 🥰 🥺 😎 🤔 😚 🤓 😴 🥵 🥶 😡 😠

Contact Info

Address
_____
_____
_____
_____

Email
_____
_____

Cell Phone
_____
_____

Wardrobe/Hair/Make-Up
*Include selfie of yourself before audition
_____
_____
_____
_____

Project / Title / Role
_____
_____

Production Company

Director / Writer

Casting

Casting Director
_____
_____

Casting Assoc.
_____
_____

Casting Asst.
_____

AUDITION TRACKER

Date:_____

- 🟩 Self Tape
- 🟩 In-Person Audition
- 🟩 Request
- 🟩 Zoom
- 🟩 Callback
- 🟩 Sides
- 🟩 Producers
- 🟩 Script

Number of callbacks ____   🟩 Booked it

MY MOOD: 😌 🥰 🥺 😎 🤔 😳 🤪 😴 🥶 🥶 😠 😡

Contact Info

Address
_____
_____
_____
_____

Email
_____
_____
_____

Cell Phone
_____
_____

Wardrobe/Hair/Make-Up
_____
*Include selfie of yourself before audition
_____
_____
_____
_____

Project / Title / Role

_____
_____

Production Company

Director / Writer

Casting

Casting Director
_____
_____

Casting Assoc.
_____

Casting Asst.

AUDITION TRACKER

Date:_____

- [ ] Self Tape
- [ ] In-Person Audition
- [ ] Request
- [ ] Zoom
- [ ] Callback
- [ ] Sides
- [ ] Producers
- [ ] Script

Number of callbacks [　] 　　- [ ] Booked it

MY MOOD: 🙂 🥰 🥺 😎 🤔 😋 🤪 😴 🥺 🥶 😠 😡

Contact Info

Address
_____
_____
_____

Email
_____
_____

Cell Phone
_____
_____

Wardrobe/Hair/Make-Up
*Include selfie of yourself before audition
_____
_____
_____
_____

Project / Title / Role
_____
_____

Production Company

Director / Writer

Casting

Casting Director
_____
_____

Casting Assoc.
_____
_____

Casting Asst.

AGENT/MANAGER TRACKER

Name	Title	Birthday
_____	_____	_____
_____	_____	_____
_____	_____	_____

Address
_____
_____
_____

Cell Phone   Email
_____   _____
_____   _____
_____   _____

Best day and time to contact
_____
_____

Other important information

AGENT/MANAGER TRACKER

DAY CALLED /VISITED	PURPOSE	OUTCOME

MY MOOD:

DAY CALLED /VISITED	PURPOSE	OUTCOME

MY MOOD:

DAY CALLED /VISITED	PURPOSE	OUTCOME

MY MOOD:

DAY CALLED /VISITED	PURPOSE	OUTCOME

MY MOOD:

CALLED INTO SAY UNAVAILABLE	FROM	UNTIL
DATE:	DATE:	DATE:

MY MOOD:

NOTES

INDUSTRY CONTACT TRACKER

Agent Connection
Name/ Agency   Date Contacted

_____

Contacted:
🟩 Call   🟩 Email   🟩 Text   🟩 Postcard   🟩 Other_____

Discussed:
_____
_____
_____

Casting Director Connection
Name/ Company   Date Contacted

_____

Contacted:
🟩 Call   🟩 Email   🟩 Text   🟩 Postcard   🟩 Other_____

Discussed:
_____
_____
_____

Industry Connection
(Director, Producer, Showrunner, Exec. Assistant, etc.)
Name/ Position/Company   Date Contacted

_____

Contacted:
🟩 Call   🟩 Email   🟩 Text   🟩 Postcard   🟩 Other_____

Discussed:
_____
_____
_____

INDUSTRY CONTACT TRACKER

Agent Connection
Name/ Agency   Date Contacted

_____

Contacted:
☐ Call   ☐ Email   ☐ Text   ☐ Postcard   ☐ Other_____

Following up:
_____
_____
_____

Casting Director Connection
Name/ Company   Date Contacted

_____

Contacted:
☐ Call   ☐ Email   ☐ Text   ☐ Postcard   ☐ Other_____

Following up:
_____
_____
_____

Industry Connection
(Director, Producer, Showrunner, Exec. Assistant, etc.)
Name/ Position/Company   Date Contacted

_____

Contacted:
☐ Call   ☐ Email   ☐ Text   ☐ Postcard   ☐ Other_____

Following up:
_____
_____
_____

INDUSTRY MEETING

Date : _____   Time : _____

Person/Company_____

Address

_____

_____

_____

In Person

On Camera

On Zoom

REASON FOR MEETING

NOTES

AUGUST

THREE THINGS YOU'VE ACCOMPLISHED AND/OR PEOPLE YOU'VE MET

THREE LESSONS YOU'VE LEARNED

SEPTEMBER

ACTING GOALS

LIFE GOALS

MONTHLY BUDGET

INCOME		EXPENSES
INCOME-1		MONTHLY LIVING
INCOME-2		
OTHER INCOME		ACTING
BUDGET		

BILL TO BE PAID	DUE DATE	AMOUNT	PAID	NOTES
_____	_____	_____	_____	
_____	_____	_____	_____	
_____	_____	_____	_____	
_____	_____	_____	_____	
_____	_____	_____	_____	
_____	_____	_____	_____	
_____	_____	_____	_____	
_____	_____	_____	_____	
_____	_____	_____	_____	

MONTHLY SUMMARY

TOTAL INCOME	TOTAL EXPENSES	DIFFERENCE

SEPTEMBER

M	T	W	T

Notes

MONTHLY PLANNER

F	S	S

Acting Priorities

_____
_____
_____
_____
_____
_____
_____
_____

Career Priorities

_____
_____
_____
_____
_____
_____
_____
_____

Life Priorities

_____
_____
_____
_____
_____
_____
_____

Positive Thoughts/Prayers/Affirmations

WEEKLY BUSINESS

ACTING　　　　　**BOOKINGS**　　　　　**PROJECTS**

SUNDAY

MONDAY

TUESDAY

WEDNESDAY

THURSDAY

FRIDAY

SATURDAY

THOUGHTS

WEEKLY BUSINESS

ACTING BOOKINGS PROJECTS

SUNDAY

MONDAY

TUESDAY

WEDNESDAY

THURSDAY

FRIDAY

SATURDAY

THOUGHTS

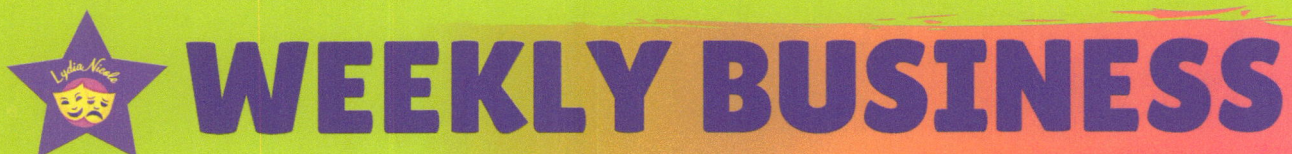

WEEKLY BUSINESS

ACTING

SUNDAY

MONDAY

TUESDAY

WEDNESDAY

BOOKINGS

THURSDAY

FRIDAY

SATURDAY

THOUGHTS

PROJECTS

WEEKLY BUSINESS

ACTING **BOOKINGS** **PROJECTS**

SUNDAY

MONDAY

TUESDAY

WEDNESDAY

THURSDAY

FRIDAY

SATURDAY

THOUGHTS

WHAT TO COMPLETE

LEAVE FOR LATER

AUDITION TRACKER

Date:_____

- ■ Self Tape
- ■ In-Person Audition
- ■ Request
- ■ Zoom
- ■ Callback
- ■ Sides
- ■ Producers
- ■ Script

Number of callbacks ☐   ■ Booked it

MY MOOD: 😌 🥰 🥺 😎 🤔 🤭 🥺 😴 😢 🥶 😡 😠

Contact Info

Address
_____
_____
_____
_____

Email
_____
_____

Cell Phone
_____
_____

Wardrobe/Hair/Make-Up

*Include selfie of yourself before audition

_____
_____
_____
_____

Project / Title / Role

_____
_____

Production Company

Director / Writer

Casting

Casting Director
_____
_____

Casting Assoc.
_____
_____

Casting Asst.

AUDITION TRACKER

Date: _____

- [ ] Self Tape
- [ ] In-Person Audition
- [ ] Request
- [ ] Zoom
- [ ] Callback
- [ ] Sides
- [ ] Producers
- [ ] Script

Number of callbacks [   ] - [ ] Booked it

MY MOOD: 😌 🥰 🥺 😎 🤔 🤭 🤪 😴 😢 🥶 😡 😠

Contact Info

Address

_____

_____

_____

Email

_____

_____

Cell Phone

_____

_____

Wardrobe/Hair/Make-Up

*Include selfie of yourself before audition

_____

_____

_____

_____

Project / Title / Role

_____

_____

Production Company

Director / Writer

Casting

Casting Director

_____

Casting Assoc.

_____

Casting Asst.

_____

AUDITION TRACKER

Date: _____

- ☑ Self Tape
- ☑ In-Person Audition
- ☑ Request
- ☑ Zoom
- ☑ Callback
- ☑ Sides
- ☑ Producers
- ☑ Script

Number of callbacks [ ]   ☑ Booked it

MY MOOD: ☺️ 🥰 🙄 😎 🤔 🥴 🤪 😴 🥺 🥶 😠 😡

Contact Info

Address _____

_____

_____

Email _____

_____

Cell Phone _____

_____

Wardrobe/Hair/Make-Up

*Include selfie of yourself before audition

_____

_____

_____

_____

Project / Title / Role

Production Company

Director / Writer

Casting

Casting Director

_____

Casting Assoc.

_____

Casting Asst.

AGENT/MANAGER TRACKER

Name	**Title**	**Birthday**
_____	_____	_____
_____	_____	_____
_____	_____	_____

Address

_____

_____

_____

Cell Phone   **Email**

_____   _____

_____   _____

_____   _____

Best day and time to contact

_____

_____

Other important information

AGENT/MANAGER TRACKER

DAY CALLED /VISITED	PURPOSE	OUTCOME	NOTES

MY MOOD: 😌 🥰 🥺 🤪 🥹 🥶 😠 😡

DAY CALLED /VISITED	PURPOSE	OUTCOME

MY MOOD: 😌 🥰 🥺 🤪 🥹 🥶 😠 😡

DAY CALLED /VISITED	PURPOSE	OUTCOME

MY MOOD: 😌 🥰 🥺 🤪 🥹 🥶 😠 😡

DAY CALLED /VISITED	PURPOSE	OUTCOME

MY MOOD: 😌 🥰 🥺 🤪 🥹 🥶 😠 😡

CALLED INTO SAY UNAVAILABLE	FROM	UNTIL
DATE:	DATE:	DATE:

MY MOOD: 😌 🥰 🥺 🤪 🥹 🥶 😠 😡

INDUSTRY CONTACT TRACKER

Agent Connection

Name/ Agency   Date Contacted

_____

Contacted:

🟩 Call   🟩 Email   🟩 Text   🟩 Postcard   🟩 Other_____

Discussed:
_____
_____
_____

Casting Director Connection

Name/ Company   Date Contacted

_____

Contacted:

🟩 Call   🟩 Email   🟩 Text   🟩 Postcard   🟩 Other_____

Discussed:
_____
_____
_____

Industry Connection

(Director, Producer, Showrunner, Exec. Assistant, etc.)

Name/ Position/Company   Date Contacted

_____

Contacted:

🟩 Call   🟩 Email   🟩 Text   🟩 Postcard   🟩 Other_____

Discussed:
_____
_____
_____

INDUSTRY CONTACT TRACKER

Agent Connection
Name/ Agency   Date Contacted

_____

Contacted:
☐ Call   ☐ Email   ☐ Text   ☐ Postcard   ☐ Other_____

Following up:
_____
_____
_____

Casting Director Connection
Name/ Company   Date Contacted

_____

Contacted:
☐ Call   ☐ Email   ☐ Text   ☐ Postcard   ☐ Other_____

Following up:
_____
_____
_____

Industry Connection
(Director, Producer, Showrunner, Exec. Assistant, etc.)
Name/ Position/Company   Date Contacted

_____

Contacted:
☐ Call   ☐ Email   ☐ Text   ☐ Postcard   ☐ Other_____

Following up:
_____
_____
_____

INDUSTRY MEETING

Date : _____   Time : _____

Person/Company_____

Address
_____

_____   ☐ In Person

_____   ☐ On Camera

                               ☐ On Zoom

REASON FOR MEETING

NOTES

SEPTEMBER

THREE THINGS YOU'VE ACCOMPLISHED AND/OR PEOPLE YOU'VE MET

THREE LESSONS YOU'VE LEARNED

OCTOBER

ACTING GOALS

LIFE GOALS

MONTHLY BUDGET

INCOME		EXPENSES
INCOME-1		**MONTHLY LIVING**
INCOME-2		
OTHER INCOME		**ACTING**
BUDGET		

BILL TO BE PAID	DUE DATE	AMOUNT	PAID	NOTES
_____	_____	_____	_____	
_____	_____	_____	_____	
_____	_____	_____	_____	
_____	_____	_____	_____	
_____	_____	_____	_____	
_____	_____	_____	_____	
_____	_____	_____	_____	
_____	_____	_____	_____	

MONTHLY SUMMARY

TOTAL INCOME	TOTAL EXPENSES	DIFFERENCE

OCTOBER

M	T	W	T

Notes

# MONTHLY PLANNER

F	S	S

Positive Thoughts/Prayers/Affirmations

Acting Priorities

_____
_____
_____
_____
_____
_____
_____
_____

Career Priorities

_____
_____
_____
_____
_____
_____
_____
_____

Life Priorities

_____
_____
_____
_____
_____
_____
_____
_____

WEEKLY BUSINESS

ACTING   **BOOKINGS**   **PROJECTS**

SUNDAY

MONDAY

TUESDAY

WEDNESDAY

THURSDAY

FRIDAY

SATURDAY

THOUGHTS

WEEKLY BUSINESS

ACTING   **BOOKINGS**   **PROJECTS**

SUNDAY

MONDAY

TUESDAY

WEDNESDAY

THURSDAY

FRIDAY

SATURDAY

THOUGHTS

WEEKLY BUSINESS

ACTING **BOOKINGS** **PROJECTS**

SUNDAY

MONDAY

TUESDAY

WEDNESDAY

THURSDAY

FRIDAY

SATURDAY

THOUGHTS

WEEKLY BUSINESS

ACTING

BOOKINGS

PROJECTS

SUNDAY

MONDAY

TUESDAY

WEDNESDAY

THURSDAY

FRIDAY

SATURDAY

THOUGHTS

WHAT TO COMPLETE

LEAVE FOR LATER

AUDITION TRACKER

Date:_____

- ☐ Self Tape
- ☐ In-Person Audition
- ☐ Request
- ☐ Zoom
- ☐ Callback
- ☐ Sides
- ☐ Producers
- ☐ Script

Number of callbacks ☐   ☐ Booked it

MY MOOD: 😊 🥰 🙄 😎 🤔 🤭 🤪 😴 😢 😬 😠 😡

Contact Info

Address
_____
_____
_____

Email
_____
_____

Cell Phone
_____
_____

Wardrobe/Hair/Make-Up
*Include selfie of yourself before audition

_____
_____
_____
_____

Project / Title / Role

_____
_____

Production Company

Director / Writer

Casting

Casting Director
_____
_____

Casting Assoc.
_____
_____

Casting Asst.

AUDITION TRACKER

Date:_____

- 🟩 **Self Tape**
- 🟩 **In-Person Audition**
- 🟩 **Request**
- 🟩 **Zoom**
- 🟩 **Callback**
- 🟩 **Sides**
- 🟩 **Producers**
- 🟩 **Script**

Number of callbacks [ ]   🟩 **Booked it**

MY MOOD: 😊 🥰 🙄 😎 🤔 🤭 🤪 😴 😢 🥶 😤 😡

Contact Info

Address
_____
_____
_____
_____

Email
_____
_____

Cell Phone
_____
_____

Wardrobe/Hair/Make-Up
*Include selfie of yourself before audition

_____
_____
_____
_____

Project / Title / Role
_____
_____

Production Company

Director / Writer

Casting

Casting Director
_____
_____

Casting Assoc.
_____
_____

Casting Asst.
_____

AUDITION TRACKER

Date:_____

☐ **Self Tape** ☐ **Request** ☐ **Callback** ☐ **Producers**

☐ **In-Person Audition** ☐ **Zoom** ☐ **Sides** ☐ **Script**

Number of callbacks ☐ ☐ **Booked it**

MY MOOD: 🙂 🥰 🙄 😎 🤔 🤭 🤪 😴 😢 😬 😠 😡

Contact Info

Address
_____
_____
_____

Email
_____
_____

Cell Phone
_____
_____

Wardrobe/Hair/Make-Up
*Include selfie of yourself before audition
_____
_____
_____

Project / Title / Role
_____
_____

Production Company

Director / Writer

Casting

Casting Director
_____
_____

Casting Assoc.
_____

Casting Asst.

AGENT/MANAGER TRACKER

Name	**Title**	**Birthday**
_____	_____	_____
_____	_____	_____
_____	_____	_____

Address
_____
_____
_____

Cell Phone   Email
_____   _____
_____   _____
_____   _____

Best day and time to contact
_____
_____

Other important information

AGENT/MANAGER TRACKER

DAY CALLED /VISITED	PURPOSE	OUTCOME	NOTES

MY MOOD:

DAY CALLED /VISITED	PURPOSE	OUTCOME

MY MOOD:

DAY CALLED /VISITED	PURPOSE	OUTCOME

MY MOOD:

DAY CALLED /VISITED	PURPOSE	OUTCOME

MY MOOD:

CALLED INTO SAY UNAVAILABLE	FROM	UNTIL
DATE:	DATE:	DATE:

MY MOOD:

INDUSTRY CONTACT TRACKER

Agent Connection

Name/ Agency   Date Contacted

_____

Contacted:
◻ Call   ◻ Email   ◻ Text   ◻ Postcard   ◻ Other_____

Discussed:
_____
_____
_____

Casting Director Connection

Name/ Company   Date Contacted

_____

Contacted:
◻ Call   ◻ Email   ◻ Text   ◻ Postcard   ◻ Other_____

Discussed:
_____
_____
_____

Industry Connection
(Director, Producer, Showrunner, Exec. Assistant, etc.)
Name/ Position/Company   Date Contacted

_____

Contacted:
◻ Call   ◻ Email   ◻ Text   ◻ Postcard   ◻ Other_____

Discussed:
_____
_____
_____

INDUSTRY CONTACT TRACKER

Agent Connection
Name/ Agency   Date Contacted

_____

Contacted:
- ◼ Call
- ◼ Email
- ◼ Text
- ◼ Postcard
- ◼ Other_____

Following up:

_____

_____

_____

Casting Director Connection
Name/ Company   Date Contacted

_____

Contacted:
- ◼ Call
- ◼ Email
- ◼ Text
- ◼ Postcard
- ◼ Other_____

Following up:

_____

_____

_____

Industry Connection
(Director, Producer, Showrunner, Exec. Assistant, etc.)
Name/ Position/Company   Date Contacted

_____

Contacted:
- ◼ Call
- ◼ Email
- ◼ Text
- ◼ Postcard
- ◼ Other_____

Following up:

_____

_____

_____

INDUSTRY MEETING

Date : _____   Time : _____

Person/Company_____

Address
_____

_____   In Person

_____   On Camera

                                            On Zoom

REASON FOR MEETING

NOTES

OCTOBER

**THREE THINGS YOU'VE ACCOMPLISHED
AND/OR PEOPLE YOU'VE MET**

THREE LESSONS YOU'VE LEARNED

NOVEMBER

ACTING GOALS

LIFE GOALS

MONTHLY BUDGET

INCOME

INCOME-1	
INCOME-2	
OTHER INCOME	
BUDGET	

EXPENSES

MONTHLY LIVING

ACTING

BILL TO BE PAID	DUE DATE	AMOUNT	PAID	NOTES
_____	_____	_____	_____	
_____	_____	_____	_____	
_____	_____	_____	_____	
_____	_____	_____	_____	
_____	_____	_____	_____	
_____	_____	_____	_____	
_____	_____	_____	_____	
_____	_____	_____	_____	

MONTHLY SUMMARY

TOTAL INCOME	TOTAL EXPENSES	DIFFERENCE

NOVEMBER

M	T	W	T

Notes

MONTHLY PLANNER

F	S	S

Acting Priorities

_____
_____
_____
_____
_____
_____
_____
_____

Career Priorities

_____
_____
_____
_____
_____
_____
_____
_____

Life Priorities

_____
_____
_____
_____
_____
_____
_____

Positive Thoughts/Prayers/Affirmations

WEEKLY BUSINESS

ACTING　　　　　　**BOOKINGS**　　　　　　**PROJECTS**

SUNDAY

MONDAY

TUESDAY

WEDNESDAY

THURSDAY

FRIDAY

SATURDAY

THOUGHTS

WEEKLY BUSINESS

ACTING **BOOKINGS** **PROJECTS**

SUNDAY

MONDAY

TUESDAY

WEDNESDAY

THURSDAY

FRIDAY

SATURDAY

THOUGHTS

WEEKLY BUSINESS

ACTING **BOOKINGS** **PROJECTS**

SUNDAY

MONDAY

TUESDAY

WEDNESDAY

THURSDAY

FRIDAY

SATURDAY

THOUGHTS

WEEKLY BUSINESS

ACTING   **BOOKINGS**   **PROJECTS**

SUNDAY

MONDAY

TUESDAY

WEDNESDAY

THURSDAY

FRIDAY

SATURDAY

THOUGHTS

WHAT TO COMPLETE

LEAVE FOR LATER

AUDITION TRACKER

Date: _____

- ☐ Self Tape
- ☐ In-Person Audition
- ☐ Request
- ☐ Zoom
- ☐ Callback
- ☐ Sides
- ☐ Producers
- ☐ Script

Number of callbacks ☐   ☐ Booked it

MY MOOD: 😊 🥰 🥺 😎 🤔 😚 🤪 😴 😢 🥶 😠 😡

Contact Info

Address

_____
_____
_____

Email

_____
_____

Cell Phone

_____
_____

Wardrobe/Hair/Make-Up

*Include selfie of yourself before audition

_____
_____
_____
_____

Project / Title / Role

_____
_____

Production Company

Director / Writer

Casting

Casting Director
_____

Casting Assoc.
_____

Casting Asst.

AUDITION TRACKER

Date:_____

- ☐ Self Tape
- ☐ In-Person Audition
- ☐ Request
- ☐ Zoom
- ☐ Callback
- ☐ Sides
- ☐ Producers
- ☐ Script

Number of callbacks ☐

☐ Booked it

MY MOOD: 🤭 🥰 🥺 😎 🤔 🤭 🤪 😴 🥴 🥶 😠 😡

Contact Info

Address
_____
_____
_____
_____

Email
_____
_____

Cell Phone
_____
_____

Wardrobe/Hair/Make-Up
_____
*Include selfie of yourself before audition
_____
_____
_____
_____

Project / Title / Role
_____
_____

Production Company

Director / Writer

Casting

Casting Director
_____

Casting Assoc.
_____

Casting Asst.
_____

AUDITION TRACKER

Date:_____

- ☐ Self Tape
- ☐ In-Person Audition
- ☐ Request
- ☐ Zoom
- ☐ Callback
- ☐ Sides
- ☐ Producers
- ☐ Script

Number of callbacks [ ]   ☐ Booked it

MY MOOD: 😊 🥰 🥺 😎 🤔 🥰 🤪 😴 🥺 🥶 😡 😠

Contact Info

Address
_____
_____
_____

Email
_____
_____

Cell Phone
_____

Wardrobe/Hair/Make-Up
*Include selfie of yourself before audition
_____
_____
_____
_____

Project / Title / Role
_____
_____

Production Company

Director / Writer

Casting

Casting Director
_____

Casting Assoc.
_____

Casting Asst.

AGENT/MANAGER TRACKER

Name	Title	Birthday
_____	_____	_____
_____	_____	_____
_____	_____	_____

Address

_____

_____

Cell Phone   Email

_____   _____

_____   _____

_____   _____

Best day and time to contact

_____

_____

Other important information

AGENT/MANAGER TRACKER

DAY CALLED /VISITED	PURPOSE	OUTCOME

MY MOOD:

DAY CALLED /VISITED	PURPOSE	OUTCOME

MY MOOD:

DAY CALLED /VISITED	PURPOSE	OUTCOME

MY MOOD:

DAY CALLED /VISITED	PURPOSE	OUTCOME

MY MOOD:

CALLED INTO SAY UNAVAILABLE	FROM	UNTIL
DATE:	DATE:	DATE:

MY MOOD:

NOTES

INDUSTRY CONTACT TRACKER

Agent Connection

Name/ Agency   Date Contacted

_____

Contacted:

☐ Call   ☐ Email   ☐ Text   ☐ Postcard   ☐ Other_____

Discussed:

_____

_____

_____

Casting Director Connection

Name/ Company   Date Contacted

_____

Contacted:

☐ Call   ☐ Email   ☐ Text   ☐ Postcard   ☐ Other_____

Discussed:

_____

_____

_____

Industry Connection

(Director, Producer, Showrunner, Exec. Assistant, etc.)

Name/ Position/Company   Date Contacted

_____

Contacted:

☐ Call   ☐ Email   ☐ Text   ☐ Postcard   ☐ Other_____

Discussed:

_____

_____

_____

INDUSTRY CONTACT TRACKER

Agent Connection

Name/ Agency   Date Contacted

_____

Contacted:

☐ Call   ☐ Email   ☐ Text   ☐ Postcard   ☐ Other_____

Following up:

_____

_____

_____

Casting Director Connection

Name/ Company   Date Contacted

_____

Contacted:

☐ Call   ☐ Email   ☐ Text   ☐ Postcard   ☐ Other_____

Following up:

_____

_____

_____

Industry Connection

(Director, Producer, Showrunner, Exec. Assistant, etc.)
Name/ Position/Company   Date Contacted

_____

Contacted:

☐ Call   ☐ Email   ☐ Text   ☐ Postcard   ☐ Other_____

Following up:

_____

_____

_____

INDUSTRY MEETING

Date : _____   Time : _____

Person/Company_____

Address

_____

_____   ☐ In Person

_____   ☐ On Camera

                                 ☐ On Zoom

REASON FOR MEETING

NOTES

NOVEMBER

THREE THINGS YOU'VE ACCOMPLISHED AND/OR PEOPLE YOU'VE MET

THREE LESSONS YOU'VE LEARNED

DECEMBER

ACTING GOALS

LIFE GOALS

MONTHLY BUDGET

INCOME

INCOME-1	
INCOME-2	
OTHER INCOME	
BUDGET	

EXPENSES

MONTHLY LIVING

ACTING

BILL TO BE PAID	DUE DATE	AMOUNT	PAID	NOTES
_____	_____	_____	_____	
_____	_____	_____	_____	
_____	_____	_____	_____	
_____	_____	_____	_____	
_____	_____	_____	_____	
_____	_____	_____	_____	
_____	_____	_____	_____	
_____	_____	_____	_____	
_____	_____	_____	_____	

MONTHLY SUMMARY

TOTAL INCOME	TOTAL EXPENSES	DIFFERENCE

DECEMBER

M	T	W	T

Notes

MONTHLY PLANNER

F	S	S

Acting Priorities

_____
_____
_____
_____
_____
_____
_____
_____

Career Priorities

_____
_____
_____
_____
_____
_____
_____
_____

Life Priorities

_____
_____
_____
_____
_____
_____
_____

Positive Thoughts/Prayers/Affirmations

WEEKLY BUSINESS

ACTING   **BOOKINGS**   **PROJECTS**

SUNDAY

MONDAY

TUESDAY

WEDNESDAY

THURSDAY

FRIDAY

SATURDAY

THOUGHTS

WEEKLY BUSINESS

ACTING **BOOKINGS** **PROJECTS**

SUNDAY

MONDAY

TUESDAY

WEDNESDAY

THURSDAY

FRIDAY

SATURDAY

THOUGHTS

WEEKLY BUSINESS

ACTING **BOOKINGS** **PROJECTS**

SUNDAY

MONDAY

TUESDAY

WEDNESDAY

THURSDAY

FRIDAY

SATURDAY

THOUGHTS

WEEKLY BUSINESS

ACTING **BOOKINGS** **PROJECTS**

SUNDAY

MONDAY

TUESDAY

WEDNESDAY

THURSDAY

FRIDAY

SATURDAY

THOUGHTS

WHAT TO COMPLETE

LEAVE FOR LATER

AUDITION TRACKER

Date: _____

- ☐ Self Tape
- ☐ Request
- ☐ Callback
- ☐ Producers
- ☐ In-Person Audition
- ☐ Zoom
- ☐ Sides
- ☐ Script

Number of callbacks ☐   ☐ Booked it

Contact Info

Address _____
_____
_____
_____

Email
_____
_____
_____

Cell Phone
_____
_____

Wardrobe/Hair/Make-Up
_____

*Include selfie of yourself before audition

_____
_____
_____
_____

Project / Title / Role

_____
_____
_____

Production Company

Director / Writer

Casting

Casting Director
_____
_____

Casting Assoc.
_____
_____

Casting Asst.

AUDITION TRACKER

Date:_____

- ☐ Self Tape
- ☐ In-Person Audition
- ☐ Request
- ☐ Zoom
- ☐ Callback
- ☐ Sides
- ☐ Producers
- ☐ Script

Number of callbacks ☐ Booked it

Contact Info

Address
_____
_____
_____

Email
_____
_____

Cell Phone
_____

Wardrobe/Hair/Make-Up

*Include selfie of yourself before audition
_____
_____
_____
_____

Project / Title / Role
_____
_____
_____

Production Company

Director / Writer

Casting

Casting Director
_____

Casting Assoc.
_____

Casting Asst.

AUDITION TRACKER

Date: _____

- ☑ Self Tape
- ☑ In-Person Audition
- ☑ Request
- ☑ Zoom
- ☑ Callback
- ☑ Sides
- ☑ Producers
- ☑ Script

Number of callbacks ☐   ☑ Booked it

Contact Info

Address

_____

_____

_____

Email

_____

_____

Cell Phone

_____

_____

Wardrobe/Hair/Make-Up

*Include selfie of yourself before audition

_____

_____

_____

_____

Project / Title / Role

_____

_____

_____

Production Company

Director / Writer

Casting

Casting Director

_____

_____

Casting Assoc.

_____

_____

Casting Asst.

AGENT/MANAGER TRACKER

Name **Title** **Birthday**

_____   _____   _____

_____   _____   _____

_____   _____   _____

Address

_____

_____

_____

Cell Phone   Email

_____   _____

_____   _____

_____   _____

Best day and time to contact

_____

_____

Other important information

AGENT/MANAGER TRACKER

DAY CALLED /VISITED	PURPOSE	OUTCOME

MY MOOD:

DAY CALLED /VISITED	PURPOSE	OUTCOME

MY MOOD:

DAY CALLED /VISITED	PURPOSE	OUTCOME

MY MOOD:

DAY CALLED /VISITED	PURPOSE	OUTCOME

MY MOOD:

CALLED INTO SAY UNAVAILABLE	FROM	UNTIL
DATE:	DATE:	DATE:

MY MOOD:

NOTES

INDUSTRY CONTACT TRACKER

Agent Connection

Name/ Agency   Date Contacted

_____

Contacted:
🟩 Call   🟩 Email   🟩 Text   🟩 Postcard   🟩 Other_____

Discussed:
_____
_____
_____

Casting Director Connection

Name/ Company   Date Contacted

_____

Contacted:
🟩 Call   🟩 Email   🟩 Text   🟩 Postcard   🟩 Other_____

Discussed:
_____
_____
_____

Industry Connection
(Director, Producer, Showrunner, Exec. Assistant, etc.)
Name/ Position/Company   Date Contacted

_____

Contacted:
🟩 Call   🟩 Email   🟩 Text   🟩 Postcard   🟩 Other_____

Discussed:
_____
_____
_____

INDUSTRY CONTACT TRACKER

Agent Connection
Name/ Agency   Date Contacted

_____

Contacted:
☐ Call   ☐ Email   ☐ Text   ☐ Postcard   ☐ Other_____

Following up:
_____
_____
_____

Casting Director Connection
Name/ Company   Date Contacted

_____

Contacted:
☐ Call   ☐ Email   ☐ Text   ☐ Postcard   ☐ Other_____

Following up:
_____
_____
_____

Industry Connection
(Director, Producer, Showrunner, Exec. Assistant, etc.)
Name/ Position/Company   Date Contacted

_____

Contacted:
☐ Call   ☐ Email   ☐ Text   ☐ Postcard   ☐ Other_____

Following up:
_____
_____
_____

INDUSTRY MEETING

Date : _____   Time : _____

Person/Company_____

Address

_____   ☐ In Person

_____   ☐ On Camera

_____   ☐ On Zoom

REASON FOR MEETING

NOTES

DECEMBER

THREE THINGS YOU'VE ACCOMPLISHED AND/OR PEOPLE YOU'VE MET

THREE LESSONS YOU'VE LEARNED

GOALS ACCOMPLISHED

IN THE LAST YEAR

GOALS

TO ACCOMPLISH THIS YEAR

JANUARY

ACTING GOALS

LIFE GOALS

MONTHLY BUDGET

INCOME

INCOME-1	
INCOME-2	
OTHER INCOME	
BUDGET	

EXPENSES

MONTHLY LIVING

ACTING

BILL TO BE PAID	DUE DATE	AMOUNT	PAID	NOTES
_____	_____	_____	_____	
_____	_____	_____	_____	
_____	_____	_____	_____	
_____	_____	_____	_____	
_____	_____	_____	_____	
_____	_____	_____	_____	
_____	_____	_____	_____	
_____	_____	_____	_____	

MONTHLY SUMMARY

TOTAL INCOME	TOTAL EXPENSES	DIFFERENCE

JANUARY

M	T	W	T

Notes

MONTHLY PLANNER

F	S	S

Positive Thoughts/Prayers/Affirmations

Acting Priorities

_____
_____
_____
_____
_____
_____
_____
_____

Career Priorities

_____
_____
_____
_____
_____
_____
_____
_____

Life Priorities

_____
_____
_____
_____
_____
_____
_____

WEEKLY BUSINESS

ACTING **BOOKINGS** **PROJECTS**

SUNDAY

MONDAY

TUESDAY

WEDNESDAY

THURSDAY

FRIDAY

SATURDAY

THOUGHTS

WEEKLY BUSINESS

ACTING

BOOKINGS

PROJECTS

SUNDAY

MONDAY

TUESDAY

WEDNESDAY

THURSDAY

FRIDAY

SATURDAY

THOUGHTS

WEEKLY BUSINESS

ACTING **BOOKINGS** **PROJECTS**

SUNDAY

MONDAY

TUESDAY

WEDNESDAY

THURSDAY

FRIDAY

SATURDAY

THOUGHTS

WEEKLY BUSINESS

ACTING

BOOKINGS

PROJECTS

SUNDAY

MONDAY

TUESDAY

WEDNESDAY

THURSDAY

FRIDAY

SATURDAY

THOUGHTS

WHAT TO COMPLETE

LEAVE FOR LATER

AUDITION TRACKER

Date:_____

- ☐ Self Tape
- ☐ Request
- ☐ Callback
- ☐ Producers
- ☐ In-Person Audition
- ☐ Zoom
- ☐ Sides
- ☐ Script

Number of callbacks ☐   ☐ Booked it

MY MOOD: 😊 🥰 🥺 😎 🤔 🤭 🤪 😴 🥶 🥶 😡 😠

Contact Info

Address

_____

_____

_____

Email

_____

_____

Cell Phone

_____

_____

Wardrobe/Hair/Make-Up

*Include selfie of yourself before audition

_____

_____

_____

_____

Project / Title / Role

_____

_____

Production Company

Director / Writer

Casting

Casting Director

_____

_____

Casting Assoc.

_____

_____

Casting Asst.

AUDITION TRACKER

Date:_____

- ☐ Self Tape
- ☐ Request
- ☐ Callback
- ☐ Producers
- ☐ In-Person Audition
- ☐ Zoom
- ☐ Sides
- ☐ Script

Number of callbacks ☐☐☐☐ ☐ Booked it

MY MOOD: 😌 🥰 🥺 😎 🤔 🤭 🤪 😴 🥹 🥶 😠 😡

Contact Info

Address _____

_____

_____

_____

Email _____

_____

_____

Cell Phone _____

_____

Wardrobe/Hair/Make-Up

*Include selfie of yourself before audition

_____

_____

_____

_____

Project / Title / Role

_____

_____

Production Company

Director / Writer

Casting

Casting Director
_____

Casting Assoc.
_____

Casting Asst.
_____

AUDITION TRACKER

Date: _____

- ☐ Self Tape
- ☐ In-Person Audition
- ☐ Request
- ☐ Zoom
- ☐ Callback
- ☐ Sides
- ☐ Producers
- ☐ Script

Number of callbacks [ ]   ☐ Booked it

MY MOOD: 🙂 🥰 🙄 😎 🤔 😚 🤪 😴 🥹 😬 😠 😡

Contact Info

Address _____

_____

_____

_____

Email _____

_____

_____

Cell Phone _____

_____

Wardrobe/Hair/Make-Up

*Include selfie of yourself before audition

_____

_____

_____

_____

Project / Title / Role

_____

_____

Production Company

Director / Writer

Casting

Casting Director

_____

_____

Casting Assoc.

_____

_____

Casting Asst.

AGENT/MANAGER TRACKER

Name	Title	Birthday
_____	_____	_____
_____	_____	_____
_____	_____	_____

Address

_____

_____

_____

Cell Phone

_____

_____

_____

Email

_____

_____

_____

Best day and time to contact

_____

_____

Other important information

AGENT/MANAGER TRACKER

DAY CALLED/VISITED	PURPOSE	OUTCOME

MY MOOD:

DAY CALLED/VISITED	PURPOSE	OUTCOME

MY MOOD:

DAY CALLED/VISITED	PURPOSE	OUTCOME

MY MOOD:

DAY CALLED/VISITED	PURPOSE	OUTCOME

MY MOOD:

CALLED INTO SAY UNAVAILABLE	FROM	UNTIL
DATE:	DATE:	DATE:

MY MOOD:

NOTES

INDUSTRY CONTACT TRACKER

Agent Connection
Name/ Agency   Date Contacted

_____

Contacted:
☐ Call   ☐ Email   ☐ Text   ☐ Postcard   ☐ Other_____

Discussed:
_____

_____

_____

Casting Director Connection
Name/ Company   Date Contacted

_____

Contacted:
☐ Call   ☐ Email   ☐ Text   ☐ Postcard   ☐ Other_____

Discussed:
_____

_____

_____

Industry Connection
(Director, Producer, Showrunner, Exec. Assistant, etc.)
Name/ Position/Company   Date Contacted

_____

Contacted:
☐ Call   ☐ Email   ☐ Text   ☐ Postcard   ☐ Other_____

Discussed:
_____

_____

_____

INDUSTRY CONTACT TRACKER

Agent Connection
Name/ Agency   Date Contacted

_____

Contacted:
🟩 Call   🟩 Email   🟩 Text   🟩 Postcard   🟩 Other_____

Following up:
_____
_____
_____

Casting Director Connection
Name/ Company   Date Contacted

_____

Contacted:
🟩 Call   🟩 Email   🟩 Text   🟩 Postcard   🟩 Other_____

Following up:
_____
_____
_____

Industry Connection
(Director, Producer, Showrunner, Exec. Assistant, etc.)
Name/ Position/Company   Date Contacted

_____

Contacted:
🟩 Call   🟩 Email   🟩 Text   🟩 Postcard   🟩 Other_____

Following up:
_____
_____
_____

INDUSTRY MEETING

Date : _____   Time : _____

Person/Company_____

Address

_____

_____   In Person

_____   On Camera

                                        On Zoom

REASON FOR MEETING

NOTES

JANUARY

THREE THINGS YOU'VE ACCOMPLISHED AND/OR PEOPLE YOU'VE MET

THREE LESSONS YOU'VE LEARNED

FEBRUARY

ACTING GOALS

LIFE GOALS

MONTHLY BUDGET

INCOME	
INCOME-1	
INCOME-2	
OTHER INCOME	
BUDGET	

EXPENSES
MONTHLY LIVING
ACTING

BILL TO BE PAID	DUE DATE	AMOUNT	PAID	NOTES
_____	_____	_____	_____	
_____	_____	_____	_____	
_____	_____	_____	_____	
_____	_____	_____	_____	
_____	_____	_____	_____	
_____	_____	_____	_____	
_____	_____	_____	_____	
_____	_____	_____	_____	

MONTHLY SUMMARY

TOTAL INCOME	TOTAL EXPENSES	DIFFERENCE

FEBRUARY

M	T	W	T

Notes

MONTHLY PLANNER

F	S	S

Acting Priorities

_____
_____
_____
_____
_____
_____
_____
_____

Career Priorities

_____
_____
_____
_____
_____
_____
_____
_____

Life Priorities

_____
_____
_____
_____
_____
_____
_____
_____

Positive Thoughts/Prayers/Affirmations

WEEKLY BUSINESS

ACTING **BOOKINGS** **PROJECTS**

SUNDAY

MONDAY

TUESDAY

WEDNESDAY

THURSDAY

FRIDAY

SATURDAY

THOUGHTS

WEEKLY BUSINESS

ACTING **BOOKINGS** **PROJECTS**

SUNDAY

MONDAY

TUESDAY

WEDNESDAY

THURSDAY

FRIDAY

SATURDAY

THOUGHTS

WEEKLY BUSINESS

ACTING **BOOKINGS** **PROJECTS**

SUNDAY

MONDAY

TUESDAY

WEDNESDAY

THURSDAY

FRIDAY

SATURDAY

THOUGHTS

WEEKLY BUSINESS

ACTING **BOOKINGS** **PROJECTS**

SUNDAY

MONDAY

TUESDAY

WEDNESDAY

THURSDAY

FRIDAY

SATURDAY

THOUGHTS

WHAT TO COMPLETE

LEAVE FOR LATER

AUDITION TRACKER

Date: _____

- 🟩 Self Tape
- 🟩 Request
- 🟩 Callback
- 🟩 Producers
- 🟩 In-Person Audition
- 🟩 Zoom
- 🟩 Sides
- 🟩 Script

Number of callbacks ⬜   🟩 Booked it

MY MOOD: 🙂 🥰 🥺 😎 🤔 🤭 🤪 😴 🥵 🥶 😠 😡

Contact Info

Address _____

_____

_____

Email

_____

_____

Cell Phone

_____

_____

Wardrobe/Hair/Make-Up

*Include selfie of yourself before audition

_____

_____

_____

_____

Project / Title / Role

_____

_____

Production Company

Director / Writer

Casting

Casting Director

_____

_____

Casting Assoc.

_____

_____

Casting Asst.

_____

AUDITION TRACKER

Date:_____

☐ Self Tape   ☐ Request   ☐ Callback   ☐ Producers

☐ In-Person Audition   ☐ Zoom   ☐ Sides   ☐ Script

Number of callbacks ☐   ☐ Booked it

MY MOOD: 😌 🥰 🥺 😎 🤔 🤤 🤪 😴 🥶 🥶 😡 😡

Contact Info

Address
_____
_____
_____

Email
_____
_____

Cell Phone
_____
_____

Wardrobe/Hair/Make-Up
*Include selfie of yourself before audition
_____
_____
_____

Project / Title / Role
_____
_____

Production Company

Director / Writer

Casting

Casting Director
_____

Casting Assoc.
_____

Casting Asst.
_____

AUDITION TRACKER

Date: _____

- 🟩 Self Tape
- 🟩 Request
- 🟩 Callback
- 🟩 Producers
- 🟩 In-Person Audition
- 🟩 Zoom
- 🟩 Sides
- 🟩 Script

Number of callbacks [ ]   🟩 Booked it

MY MOOD: ☺️ 🥰 🙄 😎 🤔 🤭 🤪 😴 🥹 🥶 😡 😠

Contact Info

Address
_____
_____
_____
_____

Email
_____
_____
_____

Cell Phone
_____
_____

Wardrobe/Hair/Make-Up
*Include selfie of yourself before audition

_____
_____
_____
_____

Project / Title / Role

_____
_____

Production Company

Director / Writer

Casting

Casting Director
_____
_____

Casting Assoc.
_____
_____

Casting Asst.
_____

AUDITION TRACKER

Date: _____

- [ ] Self Tape
- [ ] Request
- [ ] Callback
- [ ] Producers
- [ ] In-Person Audition
- [ ] Zoom
- [ ] Sides
- [ ] Script

Number of callbacks [ ]   - [ ] Booked it

MY MOOD: ☺️ 🥰 🥺 😎 🤔 🥰 🤪 😴 🥲 🥶 😡 😠

Contact Info

Address

_____

_____

_____

Email

_____

_____

Cell Phone

_____

_____

Wardrobe/Hair/Make-Up
_____
*Include selfie of yourself before audition

_____

_____

_____

_____

Project / Title / Role

_____

_____

Production Company

Director / Writer

Casting

Casting Director
_____

_____

Casting Assoc.
_____

_____

Casting Asst.

AGENT/MANAGER TRACKER

Lydia Nicole

Name	Title	Birthday
_____	_____	_____
_____	_____	_____
_____	_____	_____

Address
_____
_____
_____

Cell Phone   Email
_____   _____
_____   _____
_____   _____

Best day and time to contact
_____
_____

Other important information

AGENT/MANAGER TRACKER

DAY CALLED /VISITED	PURPOSE	OUTCOME	NOTES

MY MOOD:

DAY CALLED /VISITED	PURPOSE	OUTCOME

MY MOOD:

DAY CALLED /VISITED	PURPOSE	OUTCOME

MY MOOD:

DAY CALLED /VISITED	PURPOSE	OUTCOME

MY MOOD:

CALLED INTO SAY UNAVAILABLE	FROM	UNTIL
DATE:	DATE:	DATE:

MY MOOD:

INDUSTRY CONTACT TRACKER

Agent Connection
Name/ Agency   Date Contacted

_____

Contacted:
☐ Call   ☐ Email   ☐ Text   ☐ Postcard   ☐ Other_____

Discussed:
_____
_____
_____

Casting Director Connection
Name/ Company   Date Contacted

_____

Contacted:
☐ Call   ☐ Email   ☐ Text   ☐ Postcard   ☐ Other_____

Discussed:
_____
_____
_____

Industry Connection
(Director, Producer, Showrunner, Exec. Assistant, etc.)
Name/ Position/Company   Date Contacted

_____

Contacted:
☐ Call   ☐ Email   ☐ Text   ☐ Postcard   ☐ Other_____

Discussed:
_____
_____
_____

INDUSTRY CONTACT TRACKER

Agent Connection
Name/ Agency   Date Contacted

_____

Contacted:
☐ Call   ☐ Email   ☐ Text   ☐ Postcard   ☐ Other_____

Following up:
_____
_____
_____

Casting Director Connection
Name/ Company   Date Contacted

_____

Contacted:
☐ Call   ☐ Email   ☐ Text   ☐ Postcard   ☐ Other_____

Following up:
_____
_____
_____

Industry Connection
(Director, Producer, Showrunner, Exec. Assistant, etc.)
Name/ Position/Company   Date Contacted

_____

Contacted:
☐ Call   ☐ Email   ☐ Text   ☐ Postcard   ☐ Other_____

Following up:
_____
_____
_____

FEBRUARY

THREE THINGS YOU'VE ACCOMPLISHED AND/OR PEOPLE YOU'VE MET

THREE LESSONS YOU'VE LEARNED

AUDITION ADVICE

AUDITION PREPARATION

RESEARCH FOR AUDITION

CASTING DIRECTOR:
PAST CASTING JOBS:

DIRECTOR:
PAST DIRECTING PROJECTS:

PRODUCTION COMPANY:
PAST PRODUCTIONS:

WATCHED T.V. SHOWS/COMMERCIALS/FILMS OF WHAT THEY HAVE DONE

PREP FOR AUDITION

BREAK DOWN THE MATERIAL (SEE CHEAT SHEET ON NEXT PAGE)

WORK ON MY LINES

GET COACHED AND/OR FIND SOMEONE TO READ THE LINES WITH ME

DO MY SELF-TAPE ONLY AFTER I AM READY AND NOT ON THE FLY

AUDITION CHEAT SHEET
12 TIPS WHEN YOU GET THE MATERIAL

(DON'T BE LAZY. DO YOUR PREPARATION WITH THE SCRIPT. READ THE MATERIAL ASKING THE FOLLOWING QUESTIONS AND WRITE DOWN YOUR ANSWERS ON THE MARGINS OF THE PAGE)

1. WHO AM I? (THE CHARACTER I AM READING)

2. WHO IS THE CHARACTER I AM TALKING TO TO ME, AND WHAT DO THEY MEAN TO MY CHARACTER?

3. WHAT DO I WANT? FOR ME? FROM OTHER CHARACTERS?

4. WHERE AM I IN THE SCENE? (LOCATION OF THE SCENE)

5. WHAT ARE MY OBSTACLES?

6. WHAT HAPPENED THE MOMENT BEFORE THE SCENE STARTS

7. SCORE THE BEAT IN THE SCENE (BREAK DOWN BEATS IN THE SCENE INTO ACTIONS)

8. WHAT PHYSICAL DOINGS OR ACTOR BUSINESS AM I DOING IN THE SCENE?

9. WHERE AM I? LOCATION? (BE SPECIFIC ABOUT WHERE THE PLACE IS AND MAKE SURE TO PUT UP YOUR FOURTH WALL?)

10. HAVE I MADE HOT CHOICES IN THE SCENE? DO I NEED TO RAISE THE STAKES?

11. WHAT IS THIS SCENE ABOUT? POWER? LOVE? MONEY?

12. BE CONFIDENT IN YOUR CHOICES. NOW HAVE FUN AND PLAY!

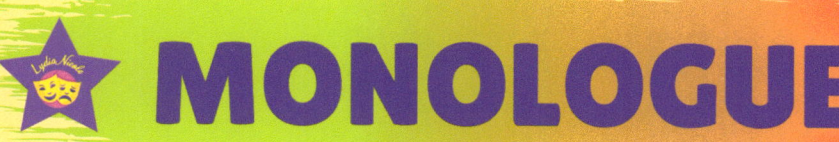

MONOLOGUE LIST

MONOLOGUES THAT HIGHLIGHT WHAT I SELL

Play/Film/TV show	Role	Description/ Genre

SCENE LIST

SCENES THAT HIGHLIGHT WHAT I SELL

Play/Film/ TV show	My Role/ Other Role	Scene Description/ Genre

TARGET SHEETS

TOP 20 TARGET CONTACT LIST

People in the business, you want to work with and build relationships with.

Name / Title	Project	Contact Info

TOP 20 TARGET TV SHOW LIST

Television shows that you would be right for.

Show Title	Prod. Co/ Producer/Casting	Contact Info

TOP 20 TARGET TV SHOW LIST

Television shows that you would be right for.

Show Title	Prod. Co/ Producer/Casting	Contact Info

TV SHOWS YOUR COMPETITORS HAVE DONE

TV shows competitors have done you would also be right for.

Show Title	Casting Director	Contact Info

TOP INDUSTRY TARGET LIST

People in the business, you want to work with and build relationships with in the future.

Name / Title	Project	Contact Info

COMMERCIAL LIST

**Make a list of casting directors/ad agencies/
commercial products you could sell and include contact info.**

Name / Title	Product	Contact Info

CREATIVE FRIENDS LIST

Create a list of friends who can help you create content.

Name / Title	Project	Contact Info

GOALS

SMART GOAL

"A goal without a plan and a date is just a wish."

Specific
Goal must be clear and intentional.

_____

Measurable
Goal must be achievable.

_____

Actionable
Must be able to take steps to make your goal happen.

_____

Reachable
This is the adjustment time when to review, revise, revisit, reflect, or reset.

_____

Time Sensitive
Add a completion date to your goal.

_____

GOALS TO MANIFEST

BREAKING DOWN AUDACIOUS GOALS
Making Manageable Goals

The goal I want:

Is this goal specific?

Why do I want to achieve this goal?

What are the steps to take to achieve it?

What skills, resources, or assistance do I need?

Why is this goal important now?

What obstacles do I see in getting this goal completed?

What is my timeline to complete this goal?

The completion date.

How do you eat an elephant? One bite at a time!

GOALS TO WORK ON

SPECIFIC GOAL/SPECIFIC TASK TO ACCOMPLISH	TIME ALLOTTED	DUE DATE	PROGRESS
_____	_____	_____	★ ★ ★ ★
_____	_____	_____	★ ★ ★ ★
_____	_____	_____	★ ★ ★ ★
_____	_____	_____	★ ★ ★ ★
_____	_____	_____	★ ★ ★ ★
_____	_____	_____	★ ★ ★ ★
_____	_____	_____	★ ★ ★ ★
_____	_____	_____	★ ★ ★ ★
_____	_____	_____	★ ★ ★ ★
_____	_____	_____	★ ★ ★ ★
_____	_____	_____	★ ★ ★ ★

GOALS TO MANIFEST

- [ ] _____
- [ ] _____
- [ ] _____
- [ ] _____
- [ ] _____
- [ ] _____
- [ ] _____
- [ ] _____

SIX MONTH GOALS

ONE YEAR GOALS

TOP PRIORITIES

_____

_____

_____

_____

_____

_____

SECONDARY PRIORITIES

_____

_____

_____

_____

_____

PRODUCTIVITY TRACKER

ACTOR'S PRODUCTIVITY CIRCLE

THE PRODUCTIVITY CIRCLE:

The purpose of the circle is to see how and where you are sending your time monthly by going back through your month and reviewing, then make a list of what you did and whom you did it with.

HOW TO USE IT:

Acting - craft, auditioning, work, creating projects,

Acting Business- social media, publicity, connecting with industry

Mind - learnING a language, reading, watching, or listening to personal improvement videos, doing hobbies, and/or doing therapy

Body- working out, sports, physical hobbies, gardening.

Spirit- prayer, meditation, etc.

Relationships - Family, loved ones, friendships, partnerships

Divide your circle into parts. There is no judgment. The purpose of this exercise is to help you see where you are spending your time and ask yourself how you can better spend your time.

Examples of divided circles into parts.

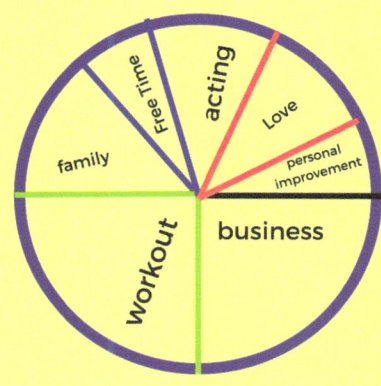
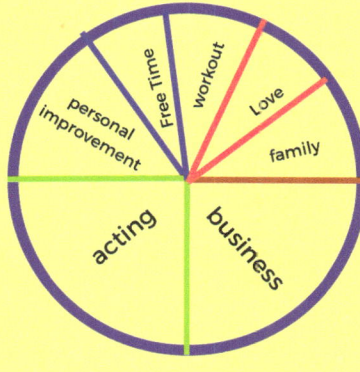

ACTOR'S PRODUCTIVITY CIRCLE

Fill it out monthly to see how you are utilizing your time.

AFFIRMATIONS & SCRIPTURES

AFFIRMATIONS WORKSHEET

1. I AM ATTRACTING _____

2. I AM LIVING A _____ LIFE

3. I AM _____

4. I AM _____

5. I AM _____

6. I AM CREATING _____

7. I AM GRATEFUL FOR _____

8. I AM COMFORTABLE IN _____

9. I AM AN AWARD-WINNING _____

10. I WIN AWARDS IN _____

11. I HAVE _____

12. I HAVE _____

13. I ATTRACT _____

14. I HAVE AN OUTSTANDING, GENEROUS, AND

SUPPORTIVE _____

15. I AM ALWAYS COMING UP WITH

_____

Lydia Nicole

The Word of God Says I am..

a child of God, (1 Peter 1:23)

a new creation (2 Corinthians 5:17)

the temple of the Holy Spirit (1 Corinthians 6:19)

delivered from the power of darkness (Colossians 1:13)

redeemed from the curse of the law (1 Peter 1:18-19, Galatians 3:13)

blessed (Deuteronomy 28:1-14, Galatians 3:9)

the head and not the tail (Deuteronomy 28:13)

above only and not beneath (Deuteronomy 28:13)

victorious (Revelations 21:7)

set free (John 8:31-33)

strong in the Lord (Ephesians 6:10)

more than a conqueror (Romans 8:37)

sealed with the Holy Spirit of promise (Ephesians 1:13)

accepted by the beloved (Ephesians 1:6)

complete in Him (Colossians 2:10)

free from condemnation (Romans 8:1)

qualified to share in His inheritance (Colossians 1:2)

born of God and the evil one does not touch me (1 John 5:18)

his faithful follower (Rev 17:14b, Ephesians 5:1)

overtaken with blessings (Deuteronomy 28:2, Ephesians 1:3)

his disciple because I have love for others (John 13:34-35)

the light of the world (Matthew 5:14)

the salt of the earth (Matthew 5:13)

chosen by God (1 Thes 1:4, Ephesians 1:4, 1 Peter 2:9)

God's workmanship created for good works in Christ Jesus (Ephesians 2:10)

healed by the stripes of Jesus (1 Peter 2:24, Isaiah 53:5)

as bold as a lion (Proverbs 28:1)

I HAVE...

the mind of Christ (Philippians 2:5, 1 Corinthians 2:16)

obtained an inheritance (Ephesian 1:11)

access by the Spirit to the Father (Hebrews 4:16, Ephesians 2:18)

overcome the world (1 John 5:4)

everlasting life and will not be condemned (John 5:24, 6:47)

the peace of God which passes all understanding (Philippians 4:7)

I have compassion and love for all men, for the love of God has
been shed abroad in my heart (1 John 4:11-12, 1 Peter 3:8,
Romans 5:5)

I WILL...

prosper, and be in health as my soul prospers (3 John 1:2)

rejoice!! For the joy of the Lord is my strength (Nehemiah 8:10)

go forward unafraid (Joshua 1:5-9)

bless and not curse my neighbor (Matthew 5:44, Luke 6:28)

meditate upon the word of God (Philippians 4:8)

pray without ceasing (1 Thessalonians 5:17)

be led by the Holy Spirit and not my emotions (Romans 8:14)

FASTING † Ideas

FROM DISTRACTIONS	FROM FAST FOOD	FROM FEAR	FROM POOR CHOICES	FROM SUGAR
FROM BAD HABITS	FROM STINKING THINKING	FROM SOCIAL MEDIA	FROM BEING WASTEFUL	FROM INSECURITIES
FROM A LIMITED MINDSET	FROM CLUTTER	FROM DOOM AND GLOOM	FROM A POVERTY MINDSET	FROM IMPOSTER SYNDROME
FROM ADDICTIONS	FROM GOSSIPING	FROM JEALOUSY	FROM UNFORGIVENESS	FROM ENTITLEMENT

IT'S A WRAP

COMPLETED AUDITIONS

AUDITION/ROLE	CASTING DIRECTOR	DATE

COMPLETED AUDITIONS

AUDITION/ROLE	CASTING DIRECTOR	DATE
_____	_____	_____
_____	_____	_____
_____	_____	_____
_____	_____	_____
_____	_____	_____
_____	_____	_____
_____	_____	_____
_____	_____	_____
_____	_____	_____
_____	_____	_____
_____	_____	_____
_____	_____	_____

COMPLETED AUDITIONS

AUDITION/ROLE	CASTING DIRECTOR	DATE
_____	_____	_____
_____	_____	_____
_____	_____	_____
_____	_____	_____
_____	_____	_____
_____	_____	_____
_____	_____	_____
_____	_____	_____
_____	_____	_____
_____	_____	_____
_____	_____	_____
_____	_____	_____

ACTING JOBS BOOKED

ROLE	CASTING DIRECTOR/ PRODUCTION COMPANY	DATE WORK DAY(S)
_____	_____	_____
_____	_____	_____
_____	_____	_____
_____	_____	_____
_____	_____	_____
_____	_____	_____
_____	_____	_____
_____	_____	_____
_____	_____	_____
_____	_____	_____
_____	_____	_____

ACTING JOBS BOOKED

ROLE	CASTING DIRECTOR/ PRODUCTION COMPANY	DATE WORK DAY(S)
_____	_____	_____
_____	_____	_____
_____	_____	_____
_____	_____	_____
_____	_____	_____
_____	_____	_____
_____	_____	_____
_____	_____	_____
_____	_____	_____
_____	_____	_____
_____	_____	_____

ACTING PROJECTS COMPLETED

WEBSERIES/ INDIE FILMS/ETC.

PROJECT TITLE	COMPLETION DATE

ACTING PROJECTS COMPLETED

WEBSERIES/ INDIE FILMS/ETC.

PROJECT TITLE	COMPLETION DATE

NEW INDUSTRY CONNECTIONS

PERSON	JOB DESCRIPTION	HOW YOU MET
_____	_____	_____
_____	_____	_____
_____	_____	_____
_____	_____	_____
_____	_____	_____
_____	_____	_____
_____	_____	_____
_____	_____	_____
_____	_____	_____
_____	_____	_____
_____	_____	_____
_____	_____	_____

NEW INDUSTRY CONNECTIONS

PERSON	JOB DESCRIPTION	HOW YOU MET
_____	_____	_____
_____	_____	_____
_____	_____	_____
_____	_____	_____
_____	_____	_____
_____	_____	_____
_____	_____	_____
_____	_____	_____
_____	_____	_____
_____	_____	_____
_____	_____	_____
_____	_____	_____

MISCELLANEOUS ACCOMPLISHMENTS

MISCELLANEOUS ACCOMPLISHMENTS

YEARLY EXPENSE REPORT

ACTING SUBSCRIPTIONS

NAME	TYPE OF SUBSCRIPTION (DATES ACTIVE FOR)	PRICE
_____	_____	_____
_____	_____	_____
_____	_____	_____
_____	_____	_____
_____	_____	_____
_____	_____	_____
_____	_____	_____
_____	_____	_____
_____	_____	_____
_____	_____	_____
_____	_____	_____
_____	_____	_____

ACTING SUBSCRIPTIONS

NAME	TYPE OF SUBSCRIPTION (DATES ACTIVE FOR)	PRICE
_____	_____	_____
_____	_____	_____
_____	_____	_____
_____	_____	_____
_____	_____	_____
_____	_____	_____
_____	_____	_____
_____	_____	_____
_____	_____	_____
_____	_____	_____
_____	_____	_____

VARIOUS SUBSCRIPTIONS

NAME	TYPE OF SUBSCRIPTION (DATES ACTIVE FOR)	PRICE

VARIOUS SUBSCRIPTIONS

NAME	TYPE OF SUBSCRIPTION (DATES ACTIVE FOR)	PRICE
_____	_____	_____
_____	_____	_____
_____	_____	_____
_____	_____	_____
_____	_____	_____
_____	_____	_____
_____	_____	_____
_____	_____	_____
_____	_____	_____
_____	_____	_____
_____	_____	_____

ACTING MEMBERSHIPS

NAME	TYPE OF MEMBERSHIP (DATES ACTIVE FOR)	PRICE
_____	_____	_____
_____	_____	_____
_____	_____	_____
_____	_____	_____
_____	_____	_____
_____	_____	_____
_____	_____	_____
_____	_____	_____
_____	_____	_____
_____	_____	_____
_____	_____	_____
_____	_____	_____

ACTING MEMBERSHIPS

NAME	TYPE OF MEMBERSHIP (DATES ACTIVE FOR)	PRICE
_____	_____	_____
_____	_____	_____
_____	_____	_____
_____	_____	_____
_____	_____	_____
_____	_____	_____
_____	_____	_____
_____	_____	_____
_____	_____	_____
_____	_____	_____
_____	_____	_____

ACTING EQUIPMENT PURCHASES

PURCHASE DATE	EQUIPMENT	PRICE
_____	_____	_____
_____	_____	_____
_____	_____	_____
_____	_____	_____
_____	_____	_____
_____	_____	_____
_____	_____	_____
_____	_____	_____
_____	_____	_____
_____	_____	_____
_____	_____	_____

ACTING EQUIPMENT PURCHASES

PURCHASE DATE	EQUIPMENT	PRICE
_____	_____	_____
_____	_____	_____
_____	_____	_____
_____	_____	_____
_____	_____	_____
_____	_____	_____
_____	_____	_____
_____	_____	_____
_____	_____	_____
_____	_____	_____
_____	_____	_____
_____	_____	_____

PROMOTIONAL COSTS

PHOTOS/PUBLICITY/ADS

PROJECT	MARKETING/ ADVERTISING	COST
_____	_____	_____
_____	_____	_____
_____	_____	_____
_____	_____	_____
_____	_____	_____
_____	_____	_____
_____	_____	_____
_____	_____	_____
_____	_____	_____
_____	_____	_____
_____	_____	_____
_____	_____	_____

PROMOTIONAL COSTS

PHOTOS/PUBLICITY/ADS

PROJECT	MARKETING/ ADVERTISING	COST

ACTING SERVICES

CLASS/ COACHING	TYPE	PAYMENT
_____	_____	_____
_____	_____	_____
_____	_____	_____
_____	_____	_____
_____	_____	_____
_____	_____	_____
_____	_____	_____
_____	_____	_____
_____	_____	_____
_____	_____	_____
_____	_____	_____
_____	_____	_____

ACTING SERVICES

CLASS/ COACHING	TYPE	PAYMENT
_____	_____	_____
_____	_____	_____
_____	_____	_____
_____	_____	_____
_____	_____	_____
_____	_____	_____
_____	_____	_____
_____	_____	_____
_____	_____	_____
_____	_____	_____
_____	_____	_____
_____	_____	_____

PRODUCTION RENTALS

PROJECT	RENTAL TYPE	PAYMENT
_____	_____	_____
_____	_____	_____
_____	_____	_____
_____	_____	_____
_____	_____	_____
_____	_____	_____
_____	_____	_____
_____	_____	_____
_____	_____	_____
_____	_____	_____
_____	_____	_____

PRODUCTION RENTALS

PROJECT	RENTAL TYPE	PAYMENT
_____	_____	_____
_____	_____	_____
_____	_____	_____
_____	_____	_____
_____	_____	_____
_____	_____	_____
_____	_____	_____
_____	_____	_____
_____	_____	_____
_____	_____	_____
_____	_____	_____
_____	_____	_____

ACTING RESEARCH

REASON	TICKET/ITEM	PRICE
_____	_____	_____
_____	_____	_____
_____	_____	_____
_____	_____	_____
_____	_____	_____
_____	_____	_____
_____	_____	_____
_____	_____	_____
_____	_____	_____
_____	_____	_____
_____	_____	_____

ACTING RESEARCH

REASON	TICKET/ITEM	PRICE
_____	_____	_____
_____	_____	_____
_____	_____	_____
_____	_____	_____
_____	_____	_____
_____	_____	_____
_____	_____	_____
_____	_____	_____
_____	_____	_____
_____	_____	_____
_____	_____	_____
_____	_____	_____

MISCELLANEOUS ACTING PURCHASES

MISCELLANEOUS ACTING PURCHASES

NOTES

NOTES

DATE _____

_____

_____

_____

_____

_____

_____

_____

_____

_____

_____

_____

_____

_____

_____

NOTES

DATE _____

NOTES

DATE _____

NOTES

DATE _____

_____

_____

_____

_____

_____

_____

_____

_____

_____

_____

_____

_____

_____

_____

NOTES

DATE _____

_____

_____

_____

_____

_____

_____

_____

_____

_____

_____

_____

_____

_____

NOTES

DATE _____

_____
_____
_____
_____
_____
_____
_____
_____
_____
_____
_____
_____
_____
_____

NOTES

DATE _____

NOTES

DATE _____

_____
_____
_____
_____
_____
_____
_____
_____
_____
_____
_____
_____
_____
_____
_____
_____
_____

NOTES

DATE

NOTES

DATE _____

_____

_____

_____

_____

_____

_____

_____

_____

_____

_____

_____

_____

_____

_____

NOTES

DATE _____

_____

_____

_____

_____

_____

_____

_____

_____

_____

_____

_____

_____

ABOUT LYDIA NICOLE

AS SEEN ON

Award-winning actress-comedienne-writer-producer, Lydia Nicole, is best known for her role as Rafaela, in Stand and Deliver. Whether portraying an illegal immigrant, gang leader, or talk show host, her ability to transform from one character to another is evident.

As a POC who found acting jobs lacking in Hollywood, Lydia took matters into her own hands and started doing standup to create more work opportunities. She began putting together her own showcases which expanded into starring and co-producing the multiracial female standup comedy show, Funny Ladies of Color (famous alums include Sherri Shepherd, Carlease Burke, Lotus Weinstock, and Karen Haber) at the World's Famous Comedy Store and Telemundo's favorite all Latina show entitled The Hot & Spicy Mamitas, which resulted in a CD by the same name. Her producing credits include NAACP Image Award Nominees Making the Five Heartbeats, In the Hive, and a Sundance favorite, Why We Laugh.

Lydia's extensive acting training includes being taught by acting gurus Stella Adler, Ivana Chubbuck, and studied under Roy London for over 8 years.

Lydia believes in service and giving back by encouraging young people whether in inner city schools, colleges, or youth prisons, as well as advising young actors on her YouTube Channel, Lydia Nicole Live.

For more information about Lydia Nicole visit www.lydianicole.com You can also follow her on TikTok and IG at @IamLydiaNicole.

www.ingramcontent.com/pod-product-compliance
Lightning Source LLC
Chambersburg PA
CBHW040438150626

46551CB00025B/133